符号中国 SIGNS OF CHINA

中国名泉

FAMOUS SPRINGS IN CHINA

“符号中国”编写组◎编著

中央民族大学出版社
China Minzu University Press

图书在版编目(CIP)数据

中国名泉 ：汉文、英文 / “符号中国”编写组编著. — 北京：中央民族大学出版社, 2024.3
（符号中国）
ISBN 978-7-5660-2276-9

Ⅰ. ①中… Ⅱ. ①符… Ⅲ. ①泉－介绍－中国－汉、英 Ⅳ. ① K928.4

中国国家版本馆CIP数据核字（2024）第017051号

符号中国：中国名泉 FAMOUS SPRINGS IN CHINA

编　　著　“符号中国”编写组
策划编辑　沙　平
责任编辑　舒　松
英文指导　李瑞清
英文编辑　邱　棫
美术编辑　曹　娜　郑亚超　洪　涛
出版发行　中央民族大学出版社
北京市海淀区中关村南大街27号　邮编：100081
电话：（010）68472815（发行部）　传真：（010）68933757（发行部）
（010）68932218（总编室）　（010）68932447（办公室）
经 销 者　全国各地新华书店
印 刷 厂　北京兴星伟业印刷有限公司
开　　本　787 mm×1092 mm　1/16　印张：9.5
字　　数　125千字
版　　次　2024年3月第1版　2024年3月第1次印刷
书　　号　ISBN 978-7-5660-2276-9
定　　价　58.00元

本册编写者

孟　石

中国幅员辽阔，有极具多样性的地质和地理区，而泉更是分布广泛、种类丰富，且数量众多。其中因水质优、水量丰或泉景奇特而闻名遐迩的名泉就有近百处之多，主要集中分布在云南、西藏、福建、广东、四川、浙江、江苏、山东、辽宁和台湾等省区。不同的泉有着不同的特点，为当地的风景名胜锦上添花：温泉四季如

China has a vast territory with a diversity of geological and geographical area, and springs are more widely distributed with abundant varieties, which are numerous. Among them there are nearly 100 well-known springs because of the water quality, plentiful water or unexpected characteristics, mainly distributed in Yunnan, Xizang, Fujian, Guangdong, Sichuan, Zhejiang, Jiangsu, Shandong, Liaoning and Taiwan, etc. Different springs have different nature, adding brilliance to the local famous scenery: hot springs are hot throughout the year; cold springs are like ice piercing to the bone; groundwater springs are as clear as the mirror; fountains are rising from the ground; geysers are mysterious. In addition, there are fantastic water and fire springs, sweet and bitter springs and mandarin duck springs, etc.

This book in the comparison form of Chinese and English introduces Chinese

汤，冷泉冰肌刺骨，潜水泉清澈如镜，喷泉动感多姿，间歇泉神秘莫测，此外还有离奇古怪的水火泉、甘苦泉、鸳鸯泉等。

本书以中英文对照的形式，介绍与泉相关的中国优秀文化以及中国名泉，并配以精美的图片，为读者展示了中国名泉的独特魅力。

excellent culture associated with springs and famous springs in China with beautiful pictures to show readers the unique charms of these famous springs.

目 录 Contents

天下第一泉

中国泉文化
Spring Culture in China

自古以来，泉水作为珍贵的水源成为人们追求的美好事物之一。茶因泉而香醇，泉水与中国的茶文化相得益彰，成为茶文化的重要组成部分。泉水因所含的矿物质成分对人体有益，泉水浴历来为人们所喜爱。历代文人墨客更是留下了许多关于泉水的珍贵墨宝与诗词佳作。

Since ancient times, spring water becomes one of the good things for people to seek as precious water. Spring water and Chinese tea culture bring out the best in each other; tea mellows because of springs, becoming an important component of tea culture. Spring water is beneficial for humans because of containing mineral substances and trace elements, and bath in the spring has always been loved by people. The ancient men of literature and writing left a lot of precious calligraphy and poetry works about springs.

> 泉与茶

水是维持生命不可或缺的灵性之物。人类与其他生物一样，离不开水的滋养。与其他生物不同的是，人类饮水有多种方式，不仅可以直接饮用，还可以以水为媒介转化饮用，如饮茶、饮酒。

茶是中华民族的重要饮品，在中国历史的发展过程中形成了独特的茶文化。中国人最早发现茶叶。传说茶叶发现于公元前28世纪的神农时代。据《神农本草经》记载："神农尝百草，日遇七十二毒，得荼而解之。"此处"荼"的意思就是茶。中国也是最早发现野生大茶树的国家。唐代（618—907）陆羽所著的《茶经》中就有关于野生茶树的记载："茶者，南方之嘉木也。一尺、二尺乃至数十尺。其巴

> Spring and Tea

Water is an essential spiritual thing to maintain life. Human being, as well as other creatures, can't do without water. Different from other living things, there are a variety of ways for human to drink water, not only drinking directly, but also making water into other drink, like tea and wine.

Tea as important drinks in China, the Chinese bred the unique tea culture in the long river of history. The Chinese first found tea-leaves; it is said that tea-leaves were found in Shennong times (twenty-eighth century B.C.). According to the *Shengnong's Herbal Classic* records, "Shennong tasted all kinds of plants in order to know functions of herbs. One day he was poisoned by 72 different poisonous plants, and found relief after tasting leaves from tea trees." China is also the earliest country to find large

山峡川，有两人合抱者，伐而掇之。”两人合抱的茶树，直径大约有1米，与1824年在印度发现的野生茶树大小相当，而时间上却要比其早了大约1100年。据不完全统计，在中国10个省区发现了近200处野生大茶树，其中以云南、贵州和四川最多，有的茶树的树龄已经达1700年左右。饮茶之风源于盛产茶树的巴蜀之地，秦汉以后开始向其他地区传播，唐代时发展至举国皆饮，故有“茶兴于唐”之说。《茶

wild tea tree. In *Tea Classics* written by Lu Yu in the Tang Dynasty, there are records about wild tea trees, "Tea is good trees in the south, with a height of one *Chi* (1/3 meter), two *Chi*, and even dozens of *Chi*. In Bashan Gorge, there is one with two people's armfuls; people cut and pick up." The wild tea tree with two people's armfuls has a diameter of about 1 meter, which is as big as the one found in India in 1824, while the time of finding it is about 1100 years earlier. According to incomplete statistics, nearly 200 places of big wild tea trees are found in 10 provinces in China. Among them Yunnan, Guizhou and Sichuan provinces own the most; the age of some tea trees is about 1700. The fashion of drinking tea originated in Bashu (Sichuan) and began to spread outside after the Qin and Han dynasties. It developed to the whole nation in the Tang Dynasty, so there is a saying, "Tea is popular in the

《神农采药图》

神农氏是中国农业、饮食和医药文化的始祖。为了分辨植物的特性，他尝遍百草。图中再现了神农身背药篓采百草的情景。

Shen Nong Gathers Medicinal Herbs

Shen Nong is the first ancestor of Chinese agriculture, food, drink and medicine culture. In order to distinguish the characteristics of plants, Shen Nong tasted various herbs. This picture reproduces the scene of Shen Nong carrying his medicine basket and picking various herbs.

• 千年古茶树
Millennium Ancient Tea Tree

经》的问世推动了饮茶习俗的流行，标志着中国茶文化的形成。

俗语言："水为茶之母"。水是茶的载体。历代茶人对茶与水关系的论述都在强调水对于茶的影响。明代（1368—1644）的许次纾在《茶疏》中说："精茗蕴香，借水而发，无水不可与论茶也。"茶叶会因水的选择而体现出不同的茶之色、茶之香和茶之味。明代戏曲家张大复重视水品甚于茶品，他在《梅花草堂笔谈》中写道："茶性必发于水。八分之茶，遇十分之

Tang Dynasty." The appearance of the *Tea Classics* promoted the popularization of tea drinking custom, marking the formation of Chinese tea culture.

There is a common saying, "Water is the mother of tea.", i.e., water is the carrier of tea. What tea tasters in past dynasties discussed to the relationship of tea and water is to emphasize the influence of water to tea. Xu Cishu, in the Ming Dynasty (1368-1644), said in *Tea Commentary*, "Perfect teas contain fragrance, discharging in water; there is no tea without water." Water choice

水，茶亦十分矣；八分之水，试十分之茶，茶只八分耳。”好茶与好水相互补益，水彰茶之醇香，茶显水之清甘，择水理所当然地成为品茶与茶文化的重要部分。

自唐代饮茶之风盛行以来，择

• **茶圣陆羽**

陆羽（733—约804），唐代复州竟陵（今湖北天门市）人。他一生嗜茶，精于茶道，著有世界上第一部茶叶专著《茶经》，被尊为“茶圣”。

Tea Sage Lu Yu

Lu Yu (733–approx.804) is from Jingling, Fuzhou in the Tang Dynasty (now Tianmen, Hubei). All his life, he was addicted to tea and was great at tea ceremony. He wrote the world's first tea monograph *Tea Classics*, and is regarded as "Tea Sage".

of making tea can differently reflect the color of tea, tea aroma and taste of tea. Zhang Dafu, a dramatist in the Ming Dynasty attached greater importance to water quality than tea; he described in his *Plum Blossom Thatched Cottage Conversation by Writing*, "Tea quality have to put up in water—less good tea in perfect water makes also perfect tea; perfect tea in less good water makes only less good tea." Good tea and good water help each other; water carries out purity and aroma of tea and tea shows clarity and sweetness of water. So water choice deservedly becomes an important part of tea sampling and tea culture.

Since tea drinking custom presented a splendid sight in the Tang Dynasty, choosing water, discussing water and judging water had become an elegant matter in the tea sector. However, due to geographical differences, as well as certain limitations of the experience and objectivity of tea tasters criticizing water, this makes people's evaluation ideas on spring water much different, producing the arguments on the "First Spring in the World", forming the tea-spring cultural diversity, and also creating a tea-spring cultural interest.

Teamen in different times have

天下第一泉

"天下第一泉"按理说应该是独一无二的，但在中国历史上被评为"天下第一泉"的就有四处名泉。一处是江西庐山的谷帘泉，一处是江苏镇江的中泠泉，一处是北京的玉泉，还有一处是山东济南的趵突泉。

The No.1 Spring in the Wold

"Normally the No.1 Spring in the World" should be the one and only, but in the history of China there are four famous springs named "No.1 Spring under the Heaven". One is Gulian Spring in Lushan Mountain, Jiangxi Province; one is Zhongling Spring in Zhenjiang, Jiangsu Province; one is Yunquan (Jade) Spring in Beijing and another one is Baotu Spring in Jinan, Shandong Province.

水、论水、评水便成为茶界的雅事。然而，由于地域的差异，以及品评人的阅历和客观性具有一定的局限，这就使得人们对评鉴泉水的观念分歧颇多，产生了诸如"谁为天下第一泉"的争论，形成了茶泉文化的多元性，也造就了茶泉文化的趣味性。

不同时代的茶人评鉴烹茶之泉有着不同的标准。"茶圣"陆羽倾向于泉水的"活"与"洁"。唐代的张又新则在《煎茶水记》中指出，泉水的"清""冷""口感佳"并配合水质"轻"为上。宋代诗人梅尧臣以

different standards of spring evaluation to brew tea. Tea Sage Lu Yu was inclined to flow and purity of spring water. Zhang Youxin in the Tang Dynasty documented his experiences in *Water Report on Brewing Tea*, noting that the clarity, coldness and good taste of spring water need to cooperate with the quality of "lightness", which is the best. The poet Mei Yaochen in the Song Dynasty took the clarity, coldness, sweetness and smoothness of spring water as standards. Xu Cishu in the Ming Dynasty, in the ariticle the selection of water of *Tea Commentary*, also took the clarity, sweetness and chill of spring water as standards. Although spring water

泉水的“清”“冷”“甘”“滑”为标准。明代的许次纾《茶疏》中的《择水》篇也是以“清”“甘”“冽”为标准。虽然

• 《林榭煎茶图》文徵明（明）
Brewing Tea in the Forest Pavilion by Wen Zhengming (Ming Dynasty, 1368-1644)

evaluation standards used in making tea in past dynasties are different, there are always two aspects of water evaluation: water quality and taste. Water quality focuses on clarity, flow and lightness while water taste demands sweetness and chill.

Clarity indicates that the spring water is clear, clean and there are fewer impurities in it. The water brewing tea should be clear without dirt so as to show tea's color and lustre. Emperor Huizong of the Song Dynasty advocated that "clear, light, sweet, and clean water is seen as the best", with clarity and cleaness being simultaneously significant and pointed out that "not to take unclean water, although it is sweet".

Flow refers to the flowing water, instead of stagnant water. This opinion

• 泉水
Spring Water

历代对用于泡茶的泉水的评价标准有所不同，但品评水之优劣无外乎两个方面：水质与水味。水质着重于“清”“活”“轻”；水味则要求“甘”与“冽”。

清，指泉水澄澈，质地洁净，水中杂质少。烹茶用水应澄澈无垢，方能彰显茶的色泽。宋徽宗主张“水以清轻甘洁为美”，以“清”“洁”并举，并指出“不洁之水，虽甘不取”。

活，指流动的活水，而不是不流动的死水。最早提出者为陆羽，他在《茶经》中言：“其山水，拣乳泉石池慢流者上。”水虽贵活，但是瀑布、湍流一类的流水气盛而脉涌，缺乏中和醇厚之气，故而被认为与主静的茶旨不合。

轻，指水的质量轻。唐代僧人允躬与宰相李德裕首创以轻重评比泉水，独钟无锡惠山泉。金代（1115—1234）的元好问参访济南七十二名泉，并记载了济南人曾取镇江中泠泉与杜康泉相互比较。清代（1616—1911）乾隆皇帝评泉也以水轻为标准，他命人特制一种银质量斗，用以称量全国各地送来的名泉水样，并亲自将之同北京玉泉

was presented by Lu Yu at first. He says in the *Tea Classics*, "When taking mountain water, overflowing spring water of newborn springs and stone pool is the best." Though live water is precious, flowing water like waterfalls and turbulence has abundant gas and pulse surge, and is short for neutralization and kind spirit, so it is not conform to tea's essence of seeking quiet.

Lightness refers to the water in light weight. The monkYun Gong and the Prime Minister Li Deyu in the Tang Dynasty first started to compare and assess springs in the term of water weight and they show special preference to Huishan Spring in Wuxi. Yuan Haowen in the Jin Dynasty (1115-1234) visited 72 famous springs in Jinan, and recorded that people there once took Zhongling Spring in Zhenjiang and Dukang Spring to compare each other. Emperor Qianlong of the Qing Dynasty (1616-1911) also took water weight as the standard to assess springs. He ordered people to make a silver *Dou* (weighing instrument) to weigh water samples of famous springs sent from different places around the country, and personally compared them with the water from Yuquan Spring in Beijing. The results showed that.

• 好水泡好茶
Good Water Brews Good Tea

水进行比较。结果显示“玉泉水重一两，唯塞上伊逊尚可相埒”，济南珍珠、扬子中泠皆重二三厘，惠山、虎跑、平山则更重，“轻于玉泉唯雪水及荷露”。玉泉水以最轻、含杂质最少被乾隆皇帝评为“天下第一泉”。泉水之轻、重类似于今人所说的软水、硬水。硬水中含有较多的钙镁离子和铁盐等矿物质，故而增加了水的重量。硬水泡茶，对茶汤的色香味皆有负面影响。

Water weight of Yuquan Spring is one *Liang* (31.25 grams), yet only Yixun water in the north of the Great Wall is the same. Water of Pearl Spring in Jinan and Zhongling Spring in Zhenjiang both are two or three *Li* (0.03125 grams) heavier; that of Huishan Spring, Hupao Spring, is much heavier. Water lighter than that of Yuquan Spring can only be found in snow water and lotus dew.Yuquan Spring water is the lightest and contains least impurities, so it is rated the "First Spring in the World" by Emperor Qianlong. Lightness and heaviness of spring water is similar to what we call soft water and hard water today.Hard water contains more minerals-calcium, magnesium ion and iron salts, thus increasing the weight of water. When using hard water to make tea, there must be negative effects to color, fragrance and the taste of tea.

Sweetness refers to delicious taste; it is the first thing to making tea. Cai Xiang in the Song Dynasty first presented that springs for tea had to be "sweet", he said in his *Tea Records*, "Spring water is not sweet, which can damage the taste of tea." If there is a bitter taste in the water, it is sure to affect the taste of tea and harm the original taste of tea.

Chill is another important standard

甘，指甘甜，为烹茶首选。宋代的蔡襄首举茶泉须“甘”，并在其所著的《茶录》中言：“水泉不甘，能损茶味。”水味若有苦涩，必定影响茶汤味道，破坏茶的本味。

冽，为评泉另一重要标准。古人记述烹茶之泉常以“甘冽”“清冽”并称。唐代张又新访泉便以此为标准。宋徽宗《大观茶论》更将其列为评鉴指标之首。

水质“清”“活”“轻”，水味“甘”“冽”的泉水无疑是烹茶用水的首选。陆羽在对各地水的经

• 《陆羽烹茶图》赵原（元）
Picture of Lu Yu Brewing Tea by Zhao Yuan (Yuan Dynasty, 1206-1368)

for evaluation of springs. When giving an account of springs brewing tea, the ancients often use chill with sweet and clear. In the Tang Dynasty, Zhang Youxin took this as the standard to visit springs. Further, Emperor Huizong of the Song Dynasty in *Grand Sight Treatise on Tea* listed it as the first evaluation index.

The spring water with clear, live and light quality, and sweet and chill taste is undoubtedly first choice for brewing tea. After the empirical study in various regions, Lu Yu summed up that water from a mountain is the best for brewing tea; river water is less good and well water is worst. "Water from a mountain" is mountain spring water, and when high quality spring water is used to cook tea, the tea color is bright, the delicate fragrance overflows and mouth feel is smooth, thus it is always the best choice for people who are fond of tea.

Spring water plays an important role in the color, fragrance and taste gain of tea, so ancient and modern masters of tea tasting had all visited famous mountains and springs, travelling over mountains and water. Where there is a famous spring, there must be a gathering place for people being fond of tea. Water is not like tea, because tea

验性考察后，总结出烹茶用水“山水上，江水中，井水下”。“山水”便是山泉水。用优质泉水所烹之茶，茶色鲜亮，清香四溢，入口滑润，故深受品茶人士的喜爱。

泉水对于茶色香味的增益具有重要的作用，故而古今品茶名家都曾跋山涉水探访名山名泉。凡有名泉之地，必定是喜茶人士汇集之地。茶方便运输，故而千里之外仍可获得，而水则不同，尤其是在交通不便的古代，并非每个爱茶之人都能求得名泉之水。故而有些喜爱品茶的文人便挖空心思，将本地泉水进行处理，以仿名泉之水。据明代的朱国祯在《涌幢小品》中记载，明代喜爱品茶的文人无法得到天下名泉惠山泉的泉水，便将一般泉水煮开，倒入水缸内，放在庭院的背阴处，待月色皎洁的夜晚揭去缸盖，让泉水承夜露，反复三次，再将泉水轻舀入瓷坛中。据说用此水“烹茶，与惠山泉无异”，故称为“自制惠山泉”。

is convenient to transport. So it can be obtained a thousand *miles* away; while water is different, especially in ancient times when traffic was not convenient; getting famous spring water was not everyone who loves tea was able to do. Hence some literati being particular about savouring tea racked their brains to process the local spring water in imitation of famous spring water. According to Zhu Guozhen of the Ming Dynasty in his *Yong Chuang Short Sketch*, literati in the Ming Dynasty being particular about savouring tea couldn't get Huishan Spring water—a famous spring in the world. So they simply boiled general spring water, poured it into a water vat, placed it in the shade of the courtyard, uncovered the cylinder head at a bright and clear moonlight night, let the spring water receive the night dew, which repeated three times, and then scooped the spring water lightly into a porcelain jar. It is said that with this spring water, one can make tea has no difference with Huishan Spring, so it is called" homemade Huishan Spring".

> 泉与保健

自古以来，养生一直是中国人极为关注的重要方面。人们通过食养、药养等各种方法来滋养身心，期望能够健康长寿，应时应季而食，则有益健康。

泉水作为独特的地理资源，因

> Spring and Heacth Care

Since ancient times, regimen has always been an important aspect that Chinese people pay close attention to in their lives. People take good care of their health through various methods such as foods, medicines and living habits.

Spring water as a unique geographical resource has long become one of the important supplements in health care, because of its gushing flow characteristics,

• 药膳（图片提供：全景正片）

药膳以中药和食物为主要材料制成，巧妙地将中药的特性、食物的味道糅合在一起，食助药力、药助食味，在日常饮食中保养身体。

Medicated Diet

Medicated diets take Chinese traditional medicines and food as the main material, skillfully mixing the Chinese medicine's characteristics with the taste of food. Accomplishing the effect that foods help efficacy of medicines, and medicines help food taste, and let people keep good health.

其喷涌的流动特征、富集的矿物质元素、因地而异的温度等，长久以来成为保健的重要辅助品之一。泉有温、有凉，不同的泉水含有不同的化学元素，故而也形成了不同的保健效果。中国利用温泉保健由来已久。历史上，人们对温泉保健功能的使用起源于秦汉，发展于隋唐，鼎盛于明清。秦始皇为治疗疮伤曾建“骊山汤”，开启了以温泉保健之先河。汉代皇帝将西域进贡的香料煮成香水倒入温泉池中，以沐香汤。隋唐皇室大兴土木，扩建华清池，并设有温泉监一职，专门负责皇家沐汤事务。当时的帝王对温泉保健非常重视，泡温泉时所使用的器物多为玉器、桃木器等，且沐浴前后的饮食都由太医特别调配，并且详细记录在册。宋代（960—1279）之前，对温泉保健的利用范围比较窄，多集中于中原及长江中下游地区，并大多局限于皇室。直至元代（1206—1368），温泉文化才扩散至疆域北部。史料记载，元世祖忽必烈曾驻跸内蒙古的克什克腾旗温泉。明清时期是温泉大发展时期，对温泉的利用基本上

enrichment of the mineral elements and various temperatures in different places. Some springs are warm, and some cool. Different spring water has different chemical elements, and forming different effects on health care. China has long-standing used hot spring for health care. Historically, people began to use hot spring for health care in the Qin and Han dynasties, which originated in the Sui and Tang dynasties, and greatly developed in the Ming and Qing dynasties. The First Emperor of Qin had built Lishan Spa for the treatment of sore wound. Since then, it held the beginning of Chinese regimen spa. Emperors in the Han Dynasty liked to take the Western tributary spices cooking into perfume and pour it into the hot spring pool and bathe in it. The royal household in the Sui and Tang dynasties built on a large scale and expanded Huaqing Hot Spring, and founded the office-Hot Spring Supervisor, being responsible for the royal bath affairs. The emperors at that time thought highly of hot spring regimen. Jade object and peach wood were often used as utensils of hot spring regimen. Imperial physicians particularly mixed diets both before and after bath, documented in the book in detail. Before the Song Dynasty

扩展到了全国各个区域，并普及到普通百姓。辽宁的小汤山温泉曾建有汤泉行宫，成为帝王宸游之地。著名地理学家徐霞客也在其旅行中发现了大量的温泉，如云南的安宁温泉等。

中国的古人们在长期的实践中，积累了大量关于温泉保健作用的资料。北魏（386—534）元苌在《温泉颂》碑文中写道：“温泉者乃自然之经方，天地之元医，出于河渭之南，泄于骊山之下，渊华玉澈……千城万国之民，怀疾沉疴之客，莫不宿粮而来宾，疗苦于斯

• 西安华清池一景

Scene of Huaqingchi Hot Spring in Xi'an

(960-1279), the use scope of hot spring regimen was relatively narrow, which was more concentrated in the Central Plains and the middle and lower reaches of Yangtze River region, and were mostly confined to the royal household. Until the Yuan Dynasty (1206-1368), hot spring culture spreaded to the northern territory. According to the historical data. Kublai Khan had the emperor's lodging when traveling in Inner Mongolia Hexigten Banner Spring. During the Ming and Qing dynasties, hot springs developed greatly, the use of springs was basically expanded to all regions of the country, and spread to common people. The imperial palace with hot spring was once built in Xiaotangshan Hot Spring, Liaoning Province, and became emperors' visit palace. The famous geographer Xu Xiake in his travel found a large number of hot springs, such as the Anning Hot Spring, Yunnan Province, etc.

Ancient people in China in their long-term practice accumulated a great deal of information about the function of hot spring regimen. Yuan Gen in the Northern Wei Dynasty (386-534) wrote in the tablet inscriptions *Ode to Hot Spring*, "Hot spring is Chinese medical classic of nature and chief medicine of

水。”北魏郦道元所著的《水经注》，作为中国古代较为完整记录河道水系的综合性地理著作，不仅记载了数量众多的温泉，还说明了其不同的特征及保健作用。《水经注》中载有温泉31个，按温度的不同从低到高分五级，依次为“暖”“热”“炎热特甚”“炎热倍甚”和“炎热奇毒”。书中还对各个温泉的特点，所含矿物质、生物等情况进行了较为详细的叙述，如有的泉有硫黄气，有的泉有盐气，有的泉有鱼等。唐太宗李世民

李时珍像

李时珍（1518—1593），明代著名中医药学家。他编著的《本草纲目》是中国古代药物学的总结性巨著。

Portrait of Li Shizhen

Li Shizhen (1518-1593) is a famous Chinese medicine expert in the Ming Dynasty. *Compendium of Materia Medica* edited by him is the summary monumental work in the ancient Chinese materia medica.

heaven and earth. It comes in the south of Weihe River, and discharges below Lishan Mountain, with magnificent, pure and clear deep pool... Hence people who have diseases, all come here to cure sufferings in the spa." *Shui Jing Zhu* (*Commentary on the Waterways Classic*) is written by Li Daoyuan in the Northern Wei Dynasty (386-534), as an integrated geographical works with complete records of river course system in ancient China, not only recording numerous hot springs, but explaining their different characteristics and effects on health care. *Shui Jing Zhu* writes down 31 hot springs, which are divided into five grades from low to high according to their different temperatures; they are successively "warm", "hot", "very hot","double very hot" and "unbearable hot". In this book, he described in detail the characteristics of various hot springs, mineral substances contained and biological conditions,etc., e.g. some springs have sulphur gas; some have mineral salt gas and some have fish. Li Shimin, Emperor Taizong of the Tang Dynasty, in *Ode to Hot Spring* recorded his experience in spa treatment to the disease, "I worry about working, and accumulate anxiousness. So I often wash in this hot spring. If not getting rid of

曾在《温泉铭》中记载了自己以温泉疗治风疾的体会："朕以忧劳积虑，风疾累婴，每濯患于斯源，不移时而获损。"明代李时珍在《本草纲目》一书中将温泉划分为热泉、甘泉与酸泉等，并论述了各类温泉的保健作用。

the disease, it will damage from time to time." Li Shizhen in the Ming Dynasty, in *Compendium of Materia Medica* divides hot springs into heating springs, sweet springs, acidic springs, etc., and explains the healthful function of each kind of hot springs.

自然疗法——温泉

温泉有着一定的保健和理疗作用。中医温泉养生的最优境界是"治未病"。养生以养为主，养则重在平时，重在顺应自然。影响人类健康长寿的因素很多，诸如遗传因素、环境因素、医疗水平、营养状况等，但养生之道重在预防。真正的温泉养生应注重养生环境，让人置身于大自然中，在山水自然中调养身心，在氤氲的水汽中体会自心本性，在清雅的环境中达到养生的效果。

• 温泉水疗（图片提供：全景正片）
Spa

Natural Therapy: Hot Springs

Hot springs have very good effects on health care and physiotherapy. The optimal state of spa regimen of traditional Chinese medical science is "preventive treatment of disease"; regimen gives priority to keep fit; keeping fit places stress in peacetime and complying with nature. There are many factors that affect human health and longevity, such as genetic factors, environmental factors, the level of medical, nutritional status, and so on, but a way of keeping good health places stress in prevention. True spa regimen should pay attention to regimen environment, place oneself in nature, take good care of oneself and exist in the natural landscape. In dense water vapor, realize the nature of one's mind, and achieve the effect of regimen in the elegant environment.

名泉
Famous Springs

在适宜的条件下，在地面与含水层或含水通道相交点，地下水能涌出地表而成为泉水。泉水因其含有的特殊矿物成分而成为人类理想的水源。其隽秀与山川的壮美相得益彰，为大自然增添了活力。中国名泉众多，分布广泛，是大自然宝贵的财富。

Spring is headwater naturally exposed to the surface after the underground water compression in the special geological environment. Because of spring water containing special mineral compositions, it provides mankind an ideal headwater. Beautiful springs and magnificent magnificent mountains and rivers bring the best in each other, and they add vigor to the natural universe. Famous springs in China are numerous and spread widely, which are nature's precious wealth.

> 玉泉

玉泉位于北京颐和园西2.5千米处的玉泉山南麓，被清代（1616—1911）乾隆皇帝封为“天下第一泉”。因泉水晶莹如玉，故而得名。又因泉水自山间的石缝中喷

> Yuquan Spring

Spring (Yuquan Jade Spring) is located in the southern foot of the Yuquan Hill, 2.5 kilometres west of the Summer Palace, Beijing. Emperor Qianlong in the Qing Dynasty confers the "First Spring in the World" on it. Because the spring

涌而出，白如雪花，曾名为“喷雪泉”。“玉泉垂虹”是金代（1115—1234）“燕京八景”之一。明代诗人王英在诗中描写玉泉“山下泉流似玉虹，清泠不与众泉同”。

玉泉出水量大，平均约为4600吨/时，有“京郊海眼”之称。又因其水头颇高，有“玉泉趵突”之美誉。玉泉与附近的迸珠泉、裂帛泉、试墨泉和宝珠泉一起组成了玉泉山泉群，经玉河、金河注入昆明湖。

water is sparkling and crystal-clear like jade, hence the name. Also because the spring water spouts out from the crack, as white as snowflake, it is formerly called Spurting Snow Spring. *Yuquan Chuihong* (Rainbows Hang down the Yuquan Spring) is one of the Eight Great Sights of Beijing (*Yanjing Bajing*) in the Jin Dynasty (1115-1234). Poet Wang Ying in the Ming Dynasty describes in the poem, "Fountain below Yuquan Hill is like rainbow; its clarity and chill are different with numerous springs."

Water discharge of Yuquan Spring is large, with an average of about 4600 tons/hour. It has a name of Sea Eyes of Beijing Suburbs. Also because of its high waterhead, it has the reputation of *Yuquan Baotu* (Baoto Spring is famous for its high waterhead). Yuquan Spring and the nearby Bengzhu Spring, Liebo Spring, Shimo Spring and Baozhu Spring together form Yuquan Hill spring group and pour into Kunming Lake via Yuhe River (Jade River) and Jinhe River (Gold River).

• 玉泉山
Yuquan Hill

• 昆明湖
Kunming Lake

颐和园

颐和园位于北京市海淀区，是中国现存规模最大、保存最完整的皇家园林，1998年被列入《世界遗产名录》。世界遗产委员会对颐和园给予了高度评价，称赞："其亭台、长廊、殿堂、庙宇和小桥等人工景观与自然山峦和开阔的湖面相互和谐、艺术地融为一体，堪称中国风景园林设计中的杰作。"

颐和园的前身是清漪园，始建于清乾隆十五年（1750年），历时15年竣工。咸丰十年（1860年）被英法侵略军焚毁。光绪十二年（1886年）开始重建。光绪十四年（1888年）更名为"颐和园"。光绪二十六年（1900年）又遭八国联军破坏，两年后重修。

颐和园占地290万平方米，划分为宫廷区和苑林区两部分。宫廷区占地不大，只是在正门处建造的一处由殿堂、朝房、值房等组成的建筑群。苑林区面积广阔，主要由万寿山和昆明湖组成。万寿山高108.9米，东西绵延1000米。南山濒临昆明湖，从山脚到山顶是一重重华丽的殿堂，这组建筑群形成了一条上升的中轴线。与这条纵向中轴线呼应的还有一条横贯山麓、东西逶迤约728米的长廊。后山则以富

• **俯瞰颐和园**
Overlooking the Summer Palace

有山林野趣的自然环境为主，兼有少量建筑物。昆明湖水面占整个颐和园面积的78%。苑林区内山环水抱，湖与山紧密地连为一体。昆明湖中的一道长堤——西堤及堤上的六座桥是有意识地模仿杭州西湖苏堤和苏堤六桥而建。湖岸和湖堤绿树荫浓，具有江南情调。昆明湖湖面被西堤与另一小堤划分为三片水域，每片水域有一个湖心岛。站在湖上西望，园内的景色和湖山浑然一体，具有一种近湖远山的自然美。

The Summer Palace

The Summer Palace is located in the Haidian District, Beijing. It is China's largest and the most intact imperial garden, and in 1998, it was inscribed on the List of World Cultural Heritage. The World Heritage Committee gave a high evaluation to the Summer Palace, praised, "The manmade landscape, e.g. pavilions, the Long Corridor, palaces, temples and little bridges, and natural mountain range and wide lakes are mutual harmonious and are artistically mixed together into an organic whole. It is called a masterpiece of Chinese landscape garden design."

The predecessor of the Summer Palace is Qingyi Garden (Garden of Clear Ripples). It was initially built in the 15th reign year of Qianlong Emperor (1750); it took 15 years to complete. In the 10th reign year of Xianfeng Emperor (1860), it was burned to the ground by the joint Anglo-French forces. It was rebuilt in the 12th reign year of Guangxu Emperor (1886). In the 14th reign year of Guangxu Emperor (1888), it was renamed "The Summer Palace". In the 26th reign year of Guangxu Emperor (1900), it was again burned to the ground by the Eight-Power Allied Forces and it was rebuilt two years after.

The Summer Palace covers an area of 2900 thousand square meters; it is divided into two parts, the palace area and garden area. The palace area covers a small area; there is only a building group consisting of palace hall, waiting room for officials and duty rooms, etc. Garden area is vast; it is mainly composed of the Longevity Hill and Kunming lake. The Longevity Hill is 60 metres high; it stretches for 1000 metres from east to west. The

south slope (front range) is close to Kunming Lake. From the foot to the top of the mountain stand layer upon layer of luxuriant palace halls; this group of buildings form a rising cetral axis. Echoing with this endwise axle wire, there is the Long Corridor of 728 meters winding from east to west, traversing the foot of this mountain. The back hill gives priority to wild natural environment rich in forest, concurrently a few buildings. The surface of Kunming Lake takes 78% of the entire area of the the Summer Palace. The garden area is surrounded by mountains and girdled by a river; the lake and mountains join closely together.The long causeway in Kunming Lake—West Dyke and six bridges on it are built consciously imitating Su Causeway and six bridges on it of Hangzhou West Lake. Lakeshore and lake dyke have green trees and dense shade with sentiment of regions south of the Yangtze River. The surface of Kunming Lake is divided into three water areas by West Dyke and its branches; each water area has a eyot. Standing by the lake, watching to the west, the scenery of the garden and the lake and mountains all blend into one harmonious whole, having a natural beauty of near lake and far mountains.

颐和园一景

从昆明湖向西望，西山、玉泉山都被借入景中。在群山的衬托下，昆明湖湖面显得更加壮阔。

Scene of the Summer Palace

Looked over from Kunming Lake to the west, West Hill and Yuquan Hill are all borrowed in the scenery. Under contrast of mountains, Kunming Lake appears more magnificent.

自金代迁都燕京城（今北京）后，玉泉山泉群成为北京城的主要水源。元代中统三年（1262年），水利专家郭守敬曾开玉泉水通漕运，初步解决了当时水源和漕运的困难。明清两代，玉泉水以水质上佳而被选为宫廷饮用水。当时政府实行严苛的宵禁制度，到了晚上就封锁城门，禁止出入，而唯独特许京都九门中的西直门在凌晨开放，

Since the Jin Dynasty moved the capital to Yanjing City (now Beijing), Yuquan Hill spring group became the main source of water in Beijing City. The third year of Zhongtong (1262) in the Yuan Dynasty, water conservancy experts Guo Shoujing set up transport for the Yuquan Spring water, preliminardy solved headwaters and transport difficulties of source and transport at that time. During the Ming and Qing dynasties, Yuquan Spring water, owing to its high quality, was elected by the court as drinking water. At that time, the government executed strict curfew system. At night the city gates were blocked off, traffic prohibited; only Xizhimen of the capital gates had the special permission to open before dawn, and let watercart loading Yuquan Spring water and inserting a yellow flag enter the city.

Yuquan Spring water is of excellent quality, providing convenience for sipping tea, brewing and irrigation. *Lianhuabai* and *Lvdoushao*, famous

• 乾隆皇帝御题的“天下第一泉”碑
（图片提供：FOTOE）
Imperial Stela of "The First Spring in the World" Inscribed by Emperor Qianlong

让插着黄旗装有玉泉水的宫廷水车入城。

玉泉水水质优良，为品茗、酿酒、灌溉等提供了便利。北京名酒“莲花白”“绿豆烧”都得惠于玉泉，皆以醇香和润、晶莹澄洁著称。用玉泉山泉水灌溉的稻米芳香四溢，成为享有盛名的“京西稻”。元代大臣耶律楚材曾特用玉泉水制墨，并命名为“玉泉新墨”，是上等佳品。

Baijiu of Beijing benefit from Yuquan Spring, which are well-known with their mellow and smooth, sparkling and crystal-clear and clean quality. Rice irrigated with Yuquan Spring water have sweet perfumes being diffused all around, and become the prestigious "West Beijing Rice". The minister Yelv Chucai in the Yuan Dynasty once made ink specially with Yuquan Spring water, called the "New Yuquan Ink", which is superior high quality goods.

- **耶律楚材**

耶律楚材（1190—1244），杰出政治家，曾辅佐成吉思汗及其子孙。

Yelv Chucai

Yelv Chucai (1190-1244) is an outstanding statesman, and helped Genghis Khan and his descendants.

> 小汤山温泉

小汤山温泉位于北京市昌平区小汤山镇内，这里素有“温泉古镇”的美称。小汤山是一座海拔仅50米左右的小山，且山麓有温泉，古人称温泉为“汤”，故名“小汤山”。这里地热资源丰富。小汤山南面在地质作用下形成一条断层线，给地下热水提供了出露地表的门径。温泉分东、西两个，两泉相距不到3米，水温却大有差异，西面的水温适中，东面的水温则高达51℃，属于高热泉。

小汤山温泉历史悠久，享有盛名。早在北魏郦道元的《水经注》中就有“湿水东经昌平县，温水注之……”的记载。自元代起这里就被辟为皇家园林，为历代帝王专享。明武宗曾为小汤山温泉留下

> Xiaotangshan Hot Spring

Xiaotangshan Hot Spring is located in Xiaotangshan Town, Changping District, Beijing City. It has long been known as Old Town of Hot Spring. Xiaotangshan is a small hill with an altitude of only about 50 meters, and there are hot springs at the foot the of hill; the ancients called hot springs *Tang* (soup), so came the name Xiaotangshan (Small Soup Hill). Here has natural advantages of being rich in geothermal resources; south of Xiaotangshan has a fault line under geological process, providing a way for underground hot water to emerge from the earth's surface. The spa is divided into two, east and west. Two springs are less than 3 meters apart, but the water temperature is much different; the temperature of the west one is moderate; the temperature of the east one is up to 51℃ , which belongs to high hot springs.

• 小汤山鸟瞰图（图片提供：全景正片）
Aerial View of Xiaotangshan

诗句："沧海隆冬也异常，小池何自暖如汤。融融一脉流古今，不为人间洗冷肠。"清康熙五年（1666年），在泉源处凿池蓄水，东西两泉泉水均流入池中，并修建了汤泉行宫。这里成为皇亲贵族前往承德避暑山庄途中休息的一个驻地。乾隆皇帝又将其扩建为前后两宫，并御笔题词"九华分秀"，还在此留下了行宫听政的佳话。晚清，慈禧太后（1835—1908）曾多次到汤泉行宫洗浴，慈禧太后浴池遗址至今犹存。

小汤山温泉泉水无色透明，泉

Xiaotangshan Hot Spring has a long history, enjoying great reputation. As early as the Northern Wei, Li Daoyuan recorded in his *Shui Jing Zhu* (*Commentary on the Waterways Classic*), "Wet water goes to east, through Changping County and hot water pours in…" Since the Yuan Dynasty, it was turned into a royal garden, exclusive for Emperors' successive dynasties. The Emperor Wuzong in the Ming Dynasty left verses for Xiaotangshan Hot Spring, "Sea is also cold in winter. Why the pool is warm like hot water? Happiness ripple flows from past till present, but it can't warm sad hearts." The fifth year of Emperor Kangxi in the Qing Dynasty

"汤泉行宫"石刻（图片提供：FOTOE）
Stone Inscription of "Hot Spring Royal Residence"

• 慈禧太后像
Portrait of Empress Dowager Cixi

水中含有钠、钾、钙、镁、碳酸氢根离子、硫酸根离子、氯离子、氟离子等化学成分，以及少量的铀、镭等放射性元素，还有大量的氮气和少量的氧气、氡气、二氧化碳等。其PH值为7.17，属于弱碱性的含氡的热矿泉水，对风湿性关节炎、神经衰弱和皮肤病等有一定的缓解作用。

(1666), a pool was chiseled to store water at wellhead; spring water of both east and west all flowed into the pool, and Hot Spring Temporary Palace was built, becoming a place for royalty and nobility to take a rest on the way to the Mountain Resort in Chengde. Emperor Qianlong then extended it into front and back two palaces, and wrote an inscription "*Jiuhua Fenxiu*", here even left a favorite topic of hearing at the royal residence. In the late Qing Dynasty, the Empress Dowager Cixi (1835-1908) had repeatedly gone to the Hot Spring Temporary Palace for a bath. The bath pool ruin of the Empress Dowager Cixi still exists now.

Xiaotangshan Hot Spring is colorless and transparent. The spring water contains sodium, potassium, calcium, magnesium, bicarbonate ion, sulfate ion, chloride, fluoride and other chemical constituents, and a small amount of uranium, radium and other radioactive elements. Still there is a large amount of nitrogen and small amounts of gases as oxygen, radon gas, carbon dioxide, etc. Its PH value is 7.17, belonging to the weak alkaline and radon-containing hot mineral water. It has a certain curative effect on relieving rheumatoid arthritis, neurasthenia and skin diseases.

> 药泉

药泉位于黑龙江省五大连池市（原德都县），是中国唯一的火山型冷矿泉，与法国维希矿泉、俄罗斯高加索矿泉并称“世界三大冷泉”。

五大连池市有由12座老期火山和两座近期火山组成的五大连池火山群。1719—1721年，火山喷发时，大量炽热的岩浆从漏斗口倾斜而下，把讷谟尔河的支流白河隔成五截，形成串珠状的五个火山偃塞湖，这就是“五大连池”得名的原因。

五大连池西南的药泉山下，有许多泉眼，被称为“药泉”。其中有四孔泉眼较为著名，即南泉、北泉、南洗泉和翻花泉。相传很久以前，达斡尔族的一个猎人在药泉山附近追赶一只腿部受伤的麋鹿，当这只麋鹿涉过药泉之后，居然腿伤

> Medicinal Spring

Medicinal Spring, located in Wudalianchi City (the original Dedu County), Heilongjiang Province, is China's only volcano type cold mineral spring, called "Three Big Cold Springs in the World" simultaneously with the French Vichy Mineral Spring and Russian Caucasus Mineral Spring.

Wudalianchi City has a Wudalianchi volcano group consisting of 12 old period volcanos and two recent volcanos. When the volcano erupted from 1719 to 1721, massive hot magma flowed down the slope from the hopper mouth; branch Baihe River of Nemor River was divided into five sections, forming five volcano imprisoned lakes with a string of beads type; this is the reason getting the name of "Wudalianchi".

At the foot of Medicinal Spring Mountain, southwest to Wudalianchi,

痊愈。于是，达斡尔族人发现了这里泉水的保健作用。每年夏天，达斡尔族人、蒙古族人远道来此，在泉边搭起帐篷，亦饮亦浴。依照风俗，他们饮前披红，以示尊重。离开时，在泉边弃石，表示将疾病和灾害留在这里。长年累月下来，这里竟形成了一座石山。

和一般火山地区的温泉不同，药泉山下的泉水是温度较低的冷泉，南泉常年水温为2.3℃，北泉水

there are many springs, known as Medicinal Spring, four springs of which are relatively famous. They are the South Spring, North Spring, Nanxi Spring and Fanhua Spring. According to legend, a long time ago, a hunter of the Daur ethnic group was chasing after a dear whose leg maimed near Medicinal Spring Mountain. When it waded Medicinal Spring, the maimed leg unexpectedly recurred. Hence, the Daur people found the spring water here having health-protective effects. Every summer, the Daur people, Mongolia people come to the spring, and build tents near the spring, drinking and bathing. According to the custom, they drape the red over their shoulders before drinking, and kill the pig to offer a sacrifice to the god to show their respect. When going back, they discard stones near the spring, showing to leave diseases and disasters there. Months and years passing by, there eventually forms a rock hill.

Unlike hot springs in general volcano areas, the spring water at the foot of the

• 五大连池火山熔岩（图片提供：全景正片）
Wudalianchi Volcano Lava

温在5.5℃左右。这些矿泉的形成与火山的活动方式和地质构造有着密切的关系。药泉山是最早喷发的火山之一，火山活动时，岩浆上升，会产生大量二氧化碳气体和挥发性物质。它们沿着断裂隙继续上升，

Medicinal Spring Mountain is the cold spring with lower temperature. Annual temperature of the South Spring is 2.3 ℃ , which of North Spring is around 5.5℃ . The formation of these mineral springs has a close relationship with the model of action of volcanos and the geological

达斡尔族

达斡尔族是中国人口较少的少数民族之一，截至2010年，约有17.1万人口。其人口主要分布在内蒙古自治区、黑龙江省和新疆维吾尔自治区，其中以内蒙古自治区呼伦贝尔盟莫力达瓦达斡尔族自治旗、鄂温克族自治旗，黑龙江省齐齐哈尔市郊区为主要聚居区。

达斡尔族的先民居住在外兴安岭以南至黑龙江以北的河谷地带。17世纪中叶以后逐步迁到嫩江流域、呼伦贝尔、爱辉及新疆等地。他们使用达斡尔语（属阿尔泰语系蒙古语族），但没有自己的文字，主要使用汉字，少数人兼通蒙古文和哈萨克文。

达斡尔族以加牛奶的小米饭和荞麦面饼等为主食，肉食以羊肉为主。他们的住房为高大的“介”字形朝南草房，内壁和天棚多有装饰，房外围柳编花篱笆。

达斡尔族最大的节日是春节，在节日里人们都着盛装，逐户拜年，妇女们互赠礼物。达斡尔族的传统运动项目是曲棍球，内蒙古莫力达瓦达斡尔族自治旗享有“曲棍球之乡”的美誉。

Daur Ethnic Group

The Daur ethnic group is one of the ethnic groups in China, and by 2010, it has a population of about 171,000. Its population is mainly distributed in the Inner Mongolia Autonomous Region, Heilongjiang Province and the Xinjiang Uighur Autonomous Region, among which the main inhabit regions are Morin Dawa Daur Autonomous Banner and Evenk Autonomous Banner, Hulun Buir League, the Inner Mongolia Autonomous Region, and the suburb of Qigihar City, Heilongjiang Province.

The ancestors of Daur ethnic group are distributed in the river valley area from the south outside of Stanovoy Range to the north of the Heilongjiang Province. After the middle of seventeenth century, they gradually moved to the Nenjiang basin, Hulun Buir, Aihui and Xinjiang, etc. They use Daur language (of Altai language family Mongolia branch), but does not have their own characters; mainly use Chinese language, a few people simultaneously are good at Mongolian and Kazakh.

The Daur ethnic group use cooked millet adding milk and buckwheat cakes as their staple food; meat is mainly mutton. Their housings are tall " 介 " shaped thatched cottage facing south; the wall and ceiling are often decorated. There are fence outside the house.

The Spring Festival is the biggest festival to the Daur ethnic group. During the festival, people all dress up to pay a new year call house-to-house. Women give gifts to each other. The traditional sport of Daur ethnic group is hockey. Morin Dava Daur Autonomous Banner of Inner Mongolia enjoys the reputation of "Hockey Town".

• 达斡尔族民居（图片提供：FOTOE）
Folk Houses of the Daur Ethnic Group

与老岩层中裂隙水相遇矿化，最后进入上部白垩纪含水层中贮存起来，在隆起区断裂处出露地表，形成次生矿泉。由于矿化时间长，且在近地表含水层中停留，故而泉水矿化度高，温度低。

药泉泉水中含有大量的二氧化碳气体和二氧化硅胶体，有钠、钙、

structure. Medicinal Spring Mountain is one of the earliest erupting volcanos. During volcano activity, magma rose, producing large amounts of carbon dioxide gas and volatile substances. Along the fracture continuing to rise, they met with the old rock fissure water and mineralized, finally stored into the Cretaceous Period upper aquifer, and

- **五大连池风光**（图片提供：FOTOE）
  Views of Wudalianchi

镁、铁和碳酸氢根等化学成分，还有锶、钡和氡等微量元素，有一定的保健价值。南泉和北泉为饮用泉，矿化度高达1.6—1.7克/升，属于铁质重碳酸盐矿泉。南泉水略呈棕黄色，清凉可口；北泉水呈微乳白色，含较多的二氧化碳气体，饮之似碳酸汽水。

南洗泉和翻花泉为洗浴用的洗泉。南洗泉位于药泉西侧，形状似

emerged from fracture surface in the bulge area to earth's surface, forming secondary mineral spring. As a result of long mineralization time and being remained in the near surface aquifer, the mineralization of water is high but the temperature is low.

Medicinal Spring water contains large amounts of carbon dioxide gas and colloidal silica, sodium, calcium, magnesium, iron and bicarbonate radical

• **药泉山二龙眼**（图片提供：FOTOE）
Erlongyan (Two Dragon Eyes) of Medicinal Spring Mountain

一个小型游泳池，夏天泉水清凉。翻花泉则位于北泉西北，因其中所含的二氧化碳气体不断汩汩涌出，翻起浪花而得名。

药泉山东南麓，还有一处水量较大的清泉，它是由两个泉眼组成的淡水泉，无色无味，清澈洁净。来此泉边洗眼，仿佛点了眼药水，因此此泉又名“洗眼泉”。

and other chemical compositions, and strontium, barium, radon and other trace elements, having health-protective value. The South Spring and North Spring are drinking springs. Total dissoloved solid is up to 1.6-1.7g/L, which belongs to the iron carbonate mineral springs. The South Spring water is slightly brownish yellow, cool and delicious; North Springs water is slightly milky white, containing more carbon dioxide gas, drunk like carbonic acid soft tasting.

Nanxi Spring and Fanhua Spring are springs for bathing. Nanxi Spring is located in the west side of Medicinal Spring, shaped like a small swimming pool; in summer, the spring water is cool. Fanhua Spring is located in the northwest of North Spring. As it contains carbon dioxide gas which constantly wells up, setting off the spray, so comes the name.

There is a clear spring of a large amount of water on the southeast foot of Medicinal Spring Mountain. It is a freshwater spring composed of two mouths of spring, colorless and tasteless, clear and clean. When people come to this spring to wash eyes, they fell as if they have taken eye drops. So the spring is called "Eye Wash Spring".

> 长白山温泉群

长白山温泉是中国著名的温泉，位于长白山瀑布北约1000米处，面积达1000多平方米。即使在严寒的冬季，温泉水依然流淌在皑皑白雪之中。

长白山是一座年轻的休眠火山，最近一次喷发距今不过300余年，所以至今仍有内热外流的现象。未冷凝的火山物质和侵入的岩浆使得地下水受热，并沿裂隙涌出地表，形成星罗棋布的长白山温泉群。长白山温泉群主要有长白温泉、梯云温泉、抚松温泉、屯温泉、长白十八道沟温泉、安图药水泉，以及天池西侧的金线泉、玉浆泉等30多个泉眼，长年蒸气弥漫，水温最高达82℃。

梯云温泉位于长白山西侧，北

> Changbaishan Hot Spring Group

Hot spring group in Changbai Mountiain (*Changbaishan*) is China's famous hot springs, located in about 1,000 meters north of Changbaishan Waterfall, with an area of more than 1,000 square meters. Even in cold winter, hot spring water still flows in pure white snow.

Changbai Mountain is a young dormant volcano. It last erupted only 290 years ago, so there is still internal thermal draining out. The uncondensed volcano material and intrusive magma make underground water heat, and pour out of the earth's surface along the fracture, forming Changbaishan hot spring group, scattering here and there. Changbaishan hot spring group has mainly Changbaishan Hot Spring, Tiyun Hot Spring, Fusong Hot Spring, Tunwen Hot Spring, Changbai Shibadaogou (18

锦江上游两岸，水温为60℃左右，属中温、重碳酸钠型水。此泉在《白山天池记》中就有记载："顺江上行两里许，江岸有汤池，曰'汤泉'。

抚松温泉在青山碧水环抱之中，水温达61℃，泉水含氧量较高，有助于缓解风湿性关节炎、神经性疾病和外伤后遗症等病的症状。长白十八道沟温泉属重碳酸钠型水，水温39℃左右。玉浆泉和金线泉直接注入天池，有诗赞美玉浆

• 长白山温泉（图片提供：全景正片）
Hot Spring in Changbai Mountains

grooves) Hot Spring and Antu Medicine Hot Spring, as well as Jinxian Spring and Yujiang Spring on the west side of Tianchi (Heaven Lake), etc., all together more than 30 springs. All the year round, steam filling the air, the maximum temperature is up to 82℃.

Tiyun Hot Spring is located on the west side of Changbai Mountains, the banks in upstream of the North Jinjiang River. The water temperature is about 60℃, belonging to the medium temperature hot and heavy sodium carbonate water. The spring is recorded in *Baishan Tianchi Records*, "Upgoing about 1 km along the river, there being a hot water pool on the river bank, called 'hot spring'. "

Fusong Hot Spring is surrounded by green hills and blue water. The water temperature is 61℃. The oxygen content of spring water is higher. It can relieve rheumatic arthritis, neurodegenerative diseases and sequelae of trauma, etc. Changbai Shibadaogou Hot Spring is a heavy sodium carbonate water; the water temperature is about 39℃.Yujiang Spring and Jinxian Spring inject directly into Tianchi. There is a poem to praise Yujiang Spring, "If you reach Tianchi, you have to pour clear spring water in

• 长白山温泉煮鸡蛋、老玉米等（图片提供：全景正片）
Eggs and Corns Boiled by Changbai Mountain Hot Spring

泉，曰："诸君若到天池上，须把银壶灌玉浆。"安图的药水泉含有大量游离的二氧化碳、重碳酸根，还含有丰富的镁、钠、钙等矿物质，泉水清澈凉爽，有助于缓解消化不良、便秘等症状。

a silver pot." Antu Medicine Spring contains a large number of mineral substances, such as free carbon dioxide, bicarbonate, magnesium, sodium, calcium, etc. The water is clear and cool, and can relieve dyspepsia, constipation, etc.

长白山美景

长白山位于吉林省东南部的中朝边界上，这里有天池、温泉、瀑布、火山遗迹、松涛林海等众多美景。

长白山天池位于长白山主峰的顶部，大体呈椭圆形，海拔2194米，南北长4.8千米，东西宽3.3千米，面积9.8平方千米，周长13.6千米，最深处达373米，是中国最深的湖泊，也是最大的火山口湖，总蓄水量约达20亿立方米。天池周围环绕着长白山的16座山峰，池水碧绿清澈，远远望去犹如镶在群峰中的一块碧玉。加上长白山瞬息万变的气候，经常云雾缭绕，天池若隐若现，如同仙境一般。

天池北侧，有一条静静流淌的水流——乘槎河，其尽头是悬崖峭壁，水流在此倾泻而下，形成了高达68米的天然大瀑布——长白山瀑布。长白山瀑布是世界上落差最大的火山湖瀑布，它轰鸣如雷，水花四溅，雾气遮天。瀑布跌入谷底，变成滚滚激流，不到1千米处便可见长白山温泉群。

The Beautiful Scenery of Changbai Mountain

Changbai Mountains is located in China-North Korea border on the southeast of Jilin Province. There are numerous beautiful scenery, such as Tianchi, hot springs, waterfalls, volcano sites and dense pine forests.

长白山天池（图片提供：全景正片）
Tianchi (Heaven Lake) of Changbai Mountains

Tianchi (Heaven Lake) of Changbai Mountains is located on the top of Baitou Mountain, which is the main peak of Changbai Mountains. It roughly appears the ellipse, being the height of 2194 meters, 4.8 km long from north to south, 3.3 km wide from east to west, with an area of 9.8 square kilometers, 13.6 km circumference. The maximum depth of 373 meters, it is the deepest lake and the largest volcano crater lake in China. The gross storage capacity is about 2 billion cubic meters. 16 mountain peaks of Changbai Mountains surround Tianchi; the water of which is green and clear. It looks like a piece of jade inlaid in the peaks from a distance. With the climate varying from minute to minute of Changbai Mountains, cloud and mist often curl up, so Tianchi is partly hidden and partly visible, like a fairyland in general.

On the north side of Tianchi, there is a quietly flowing water flow-Chengcha River, the end of which is precipitous rock faces and sheer cliffs, water flow pouring down here, forming up to 68 meters of natural falls Changbaishan Waterfall. Changbaishan Waterfall is the world's volcano lake falls of the largest waterfall drop. It roars like thunder. The water splashes in all directions, and mists cover the sky. The waterfall falls into the valley, becoming billowing riptide. Changbaishan hot spring group can be seen less than 1 km.

> 汤岗子温泉

汤岗子温泉位于辽宁鞍山市南7.5千米处。古人常称温泉为“汤”，而此地周围又有山岗子，便名为“汤岗子”。

汤岗子温泉历史悠久，据《海

• 汤岗子温泉旅游度假区的唐王浴泉雕塑（图片提供：FOTOE）
Sculpture of Emperor Taizong in the Tang Dynasty Bathing in Spring in Hot Springs Tourism Holiday Resort of Tanggangzi Hot Spring

> Tanggangzi Hot Spring

Tanggangzi Hot Spring is 7.5 km south of Anshan City, Liaoning Province. The ancients often called hot spring "*Tang* (soup)", and it is surrounded by hills, so called "*Tanggangzi*".

Tanggangzi Hot Spring has a long history. According to *Haicheng County Annals*, as early as in the 18th year of Zhenguan Period (644), people found and used it. Aaccording to legend, when Emperor Taizong of the Tang Dynasty Li Shimin went on a punitive expedition east for Koguryo, he had a bath here. The 8th year of Tianhui Period (1130), Emperor Taizong of Jin had a bath out of admiration for the spring. Tangchi County was especially set up here during the Liao and Jin dynasties. After the Ming and Qing dynasties, "Making room above it, bathers came one after the other."

• **千山风景区灵岩寺**（图片提供：FOTOE）

千山因群峰耸立宛如千朵莲花，又名“千朵莲花山”，被誉为东北诸山之冠。由于千山地势奇险峭立，远在隋唐时期，此地便开始修建庙宇，后来，庙宇越来越多，至今仍有许多庙宇保存完整。汤岗子温泉便在千山风景区内，名泉加上胜景，绚丽多姿。

Lingyan Temple in Qianshan Scenic Spot

Because towering peaks of Qianshan Mountain are just like a thousand lotus flowers, it is also known as "Thousand Lotus Flowers Hill", and it is reputed to the crown of various mountains in Northeast. As the Qianshan Mountain terrain is strategically located and difficult of access and rising steeply, as far back as the Sui and Tang dynasties, temples began to be built here. Afterwards the temples are more and more, and there are still many well-preserved temples so far. Tanggangzi Hot Spring is just in the Qianshan Scenic Spot. Hot springs and wonderful scenery are gorgeous and colorful.

城县志》记载，其早在唐朝贞观十八年（644年）即被人们发现并利用。相传唐太宗李世民东征高句丽时，曾在此“坐汤”（沐浴）天会八年（1130年），金太宗也慕名前来沐浴。辽金时期在此特设汤池县。明清以后，“筑室其上，沐浴者络绎不绝”。

Tanggangzi has originally 18 hot springs; spring water pours out from underground granite cracks; daily water yield is more than 1000 tons, and the water temperature is 57℃-72℃. Currently mouths of hot springs are replaced by manual built pipelines. Spring water is clear and transparent, colorless and tasteless, containing oxygen, fluorine,

汤岗子地区原有18处温泉，泉水从地下花岗岩裂隙中涌出，每日涌水量达1000多吨，水温57℃—72℃。目前温泉泉眼已被人工修筑的管道代替。泉水清澈透明、无色无味，含氧、氟、二氧化硅、钠、硫酸盐和氮气等。特别是水中还含有氡气（一种具有微弱放射性的惰性气体，是镭在衰变过程中的产物），有一定的保健价值。

汤岗子地区的热矿泥、矿泉蕴藏丰富。热矿泥的深度达四五十米，范围比矿泉分布面积大2.5倍。热矿泥独具特色，为迄今亚洲唯一的温度高达45℃的湿润泥土。经国家地质部门考证，热矿泥是数亿年前的火山爆发形成的火山灰的沉积物，经过近亿年的温泉滋养和理化作用而形成的。热矿泥颗粒均匀、柔软细腻，对治疗风湿、类风湿、关节炎、神经衰弱、软组织损伤及解除疲劳等均有益处。

silicon dioxide, sodium, sulfate and nitrogen. Especially the water also contains radon (an inert gas having weak radioactivity, which is the product of radium in its radioactive disintegration process), having health proteetive value.

Tanggangzi contains rich hot slime and mineral springs. Hot slime has a depth of up to forty or fifty meters; the range is 2.5 times larger than the mineral spring distribution area. Hot slime is unique, and so far it is the only Asian moist soil with a temperature of up to 45℃. By the research of national geological department, hot slime is volcano ash sediments after the outbreak of volcano hundreds of millions of years ago, forming after nearly a hundred million years, under the physico-chemical function of hot spring nourishing. Hot slime is of uniform particles, soft and exquisite, having effects on reliveving rheumatism, rheumatoid, arthritis, neurasthenia, soft tissue injury and the alleviating of fatigue.

> 热河泉

热河泉位于河北承德避暑山庄内湖区的东北隅。湖畔立着一块自然石，上面刻着清代道光皇帝亲题的“热河”两个大字。这里是热河泉的源头，清澈的泉水由地下涌

• 刻有“热河”二字的自然石（图片提供：全景正片）
Natural Stone Engraved with Two Big Characters *Rehe*

> Rehe Spring

Rehe Spring is located in the northeast corner of Lakes Region in the Mountain Resort in Chengde, Hebei Province. A natural stone stands beside the lake, two big characters *Rehe* engraved on it, which is personally inscribed by the Emperor Daoguang of the Qing Dynasty. Here is the Rehe Spring source, where clear spring water gushes from underground, through the Chenghu Lake, Ruyi Lake, Upper Lake and Lower Lake, flows out from five hole floodgates on south of Yin Lake, and enters Wulie River along the long embankments; the overall length is about 700 meters. Rehe Spring was once regarded as a river, and was regarded as the world's shortest River in *Encyclopedia Britannica*. But precisely, it is only a spring, not a river, and in 1979, it is officially named Rehe Spring.

出，流经澄湖、如意湖、上湖、下湖，自银湖南部的五孔闸流出，沿长堤汇入武烈河，全长700多米。热河泉曾被当作河，并被当作世界最短的河列入《大英百科全书》。但是准确地说，热河只是一个泉，而非河流，1979年被正式定名为“热河泉”。

热河泉是避暑山庄内湖泊的主要水源，泉流四涌，汇成碧波千顷。热河泉一年四季胜景不衰。春季，位于泉水源头的澄湖清澈见

Rehe Spring is the main source of water of the lakes in the Mountain Resort, stream of spring water gushing all around, merging into a vast lake with blue waves; the source is distant and the stream is long. The beautiful scenery of Rehe Spring does not fade all the year round. In spring, Chenghu Lake is water of spring water source is transparently clear and limpid with swimming fish; in summer, dots of duckweed scatter on the water surface; in autumn, the temperature of spring water is high, and lotuses are blooming with the autumn

• 承德避暑山庄内湖荷叶飘香

Inner Lake Lotus Leaves Drifting Fragrance in the Mountain Resort in Chengde

底，游鱼戏水；夏季，绿萍点点，漂浮水面；秋季，泉水水温较高，荷花与秋菊、寒梅争艳；冬季，整个山庄被白雪覆盖，湖面结冰尺余，唯有澄湖水面仍是碧水涟漪，雾霭蒸腾，堪为奇观。

chrysanthemum and the plum blossom; in winter, the whole Imperial Summer Villa is covered with white snow, and the lake ice is more than 0.3 m; only the surface of Chenghu Lake is still rippling blue water with mist transpiration, which can indeed be a wonder.

承德避暑山庄

避暑山庄位于河北承德北部，又名“承德离宫”或“热河行宫”，是清代皇帝夏天避暑和处理政务的场所。其始建于康熙四十二年（1703年），历经康熙、雍正、乾隆三朝，耗时近90年建成。

• 承德避暑山庄松鹤斋
Pine and Crane Room (*Songhe Zhai*) in the Mountain Resort in Chengde

• 承德避暑山庄外八庙之普宁寺
Runing Temple in the Mountain Resort in Chengde

避暑山庄占地面积560余万平方米，是中国现存最大的古典皇家园林。其与北京的颐和园、苏州的拙政园和留园并称中国四大名园。1994年12月，避暑山庄和周围寺庙被列入《世界遗产名录》。世界遗产委员会对其的评价为："它是由众多的宫殿以及其他处理政务、举行仪式的建筑构成的一个庞大的建筑群。建筑风格各异的庙宇和皇家园林同周围的湖泊、牧场和森林巧妙地融为一体。避暑山庄不仅具有极高的美学研究价值，而且还保留着中国封建社会发展末期的罕见的历史遗迹。"

The Mountain Resort in Chengde

The Mountain Resort in Chengde was called Rehe Palace in history, conventionally known as Chengde *Ligong* (a temporary abode for an emperor on progresses). Located in northern Chengde, Hebei Province, it was a place for Emperors of the Qing Dynasty to be away for the summer holidays and to handle government affairs in summer. The construction started in the

42th reign year of Kangxi Emperor (1703), through reigns of Kangxi, Yongzheng and Qianlong, consuming nearly 90 years to complete.

The Mountain Resort covers an area of more than 5.6 million square meters; it is the largest existing classical royal gardens in China. The the Mountain Resort, the Summer Palace in Beijing, Humble Administrator's Garden and Lingering Garden in Suzhou are called Four Famous Gardens in China. In December, 1994, the Mountain Resort and surrounding temples were inscribed on the World Heritage List. The World Heritage Committee gave it the evaluation, "It is a huge building group composed of numerous palaces and other buildings handling government affairs and holding ceremonies. Temples of various architectural styles and royal family garden blend skillfully into the surrounding lakes, meadows and forest. The Mountain Resort not only has a very high aesthetic value, but also continues to have rare historical relics of the final development of feudal society in China."

热河泉的形成与古老的火山运动有关。约在7000万年前，承德地区曾发生过规模巨大的火山喷发。火山岩浆沿岩层裂隙溢出，岩层出现了许多断裂隙。地面上的水通过裂隙深入地壳深处，经地热加温后，水温升高，再沿燕山断裂带的缝隙等处涌出地表。热河泉的水温虽只有9℃—17℃，但仍高于当地的年平均气温（8.8℃），在冬天可泛出热气，所以可称为“温泉”。泉水中含较多的碳酸钙、碳酸镁，但矿化度很低。水中还含有少量可溶性二氧化碳、微量的氟和硼酸，口感甘甜、清凉、爽口。

The formation of Rehe Spring has something to do with ancient volcano movement. About 70 million years ago, a tremendous volcano eruption once occurred in Chengde area. Volcano magma overflowed along the rock crack; rock stratum appeared many faulted joint; water above ground got deep into the earth crust through faulted joint. After heated by terrestrial heat, water temperature went up, then water gushed out to the surface along the cracks of Yanshan Mountain fracture zone. The temperature of hot spring water is only 9℃-17℃, but still higher than the local average annual temperature (8.8℃). Especially in winter, hot gas can drift

• 俯视承德避暑山庄一景

Overlooking at the Scene of the Mountain Resort in Chengde

out, so it can be called "hot spring". Spring water contains more calcium carbonate and magnesium carbonate, but the mineralization of water is very low. The water also contains a small amount of soluble carbon dioxide, insignificant amounts of fluorine and boric acid. The mouthfeel is sweet, cool, tasty and refreshing.

> 趵突泉

趵突泉位于山东省济南市的中心，南靠千佛山，北望大明湖。其“三泉喷涌，势若鼎沸，状似堆雪”，更被誉为济南七十二名泉之首，曾被乾隆皇帝御封为“天下第一泉”。

有关学者据河南安阳出土的甲骨文考证，趵突泉有文字记载的历史可上溯至商代（前1600—前1046）。趵突泉古时称“泺”，在2600余年前的编年史《春秋》中便

> Baotu Spring

Baotu Spring is located in the center of Jinan, Shandong Province, south to Qianfo Mountain, north to Daming Lake. Due to its "three springs gushing, supercharged potential force and shaped like a pile of snow",the spring is further rank with the first of the seventy-two famous springs in Jinan, which was formerly conferred the "Number One Spring in the World" by Emperor Qianlong of the Qing Dynasty.

According to relevant scholars' textual criticism to the oracle bone

济南趵突泉（图片提供：全景正片）
Baotu Spring of Jinan

济南七十二名泉

济南有“泉城”的美誉，号称有七十二名泉。其实济南的泉眼数量远不止此数，历代的文献记载也各不相同，连当地人也难以说出确切的数字。正如清末小说家刘鹗在《老残游记》中所言，济南是“家家泉水，户户垂杨”。济南多泉水与其地理位置和地质构造有关。济南地势南高北低，地下水由南向北流动。济南南部广大的山区为石灰岩构造，容易形成裂隙和溶洞，而大明湖以北为坚硬且不易透水的火成岩，水流的通道被阻，自然沿裂隙涌出地表，这就形成了泉水。

按照众多泉眼分布和汇流的情况，济南的泉水大概可分为四大泉群：趵突泉群、珍珠泉群、黑虎泉群和五龙潭泉群。泉水千姿百态，或银流翻滚，或珠串玉连，或忽断忽续，或忽隐忽现。其中趵突泉、黑虎泉、珍珠泉和金线泉并称为济南市四大名泉。

Seventy-two Famous Springs in Jinan

Jinan has the reputation of "Spring City", known for having seventy-two famous springs. But in fact, the number of springs in Jinan is far more than this; historical document records are not

• 济南大明湖（图片提供：全景正片）
Daming Lake of Jinan

identical, even the locals also can't accurately tell the exact number. Just as what the novelist Liu E in the late Qing Dynasty said in *the Travels of Lao Ts'an*, Jinan is in a condition that "every family has spring water and every household has drooping willows". The cause of these springs has something to do with its geographical location and structure. The terrain of Jinan is higher in south and lower in north, causing groundwater to flow northward; the south of the vast mountains is of limestone structure, easy to form fractures and karst caves, while the north of Daming Lake is hard and not easily permeable igneous rocks. Water flow passageways are blocked, and it naturally come out of surface and forms springs along the fissures.

According to the circumstances of concentration and confluence of the numerous springs distribution, maybe Jinan springs can be divided into four big spring groups: Baotu Spring group, Zhenzhu (pearl) Spring group, Heihu (black tiger) Spring group and Wulongtan (five dragons' deep pool) Spring group. All springs are in different poses and with different expressions, or silver stream tumbling, or beading pearls and joining jade, or suddenly breaking and suddenly adding, or suddenly hiding and suddenly appearing. Among them, Baotu Spring, Heihu Spring, Zhenzhu Spring and Jinxian (golden threads) Spring are known together as the Four Most Famous Springs of Jinan City.

有"（鲁桓）公会齐侯于泺"的记载。宋代散文家曾巩任齐州知州时，在泉边建泺源堂，并赋予泺水"趵突泉"的名称。"趵突"，即跳跃奔突之意，反映了趵突泉三泉迸发、喷涌不息的特点。"趵突"不仅字面古雅，而且音义兼顾，既以"趵突"形容泉水跳跃之状、喷涌不息之动态，又以"趵突"模拟泉水喷涌时的声音。

趵突泉的泉水自三穴喷涌而出汇水成潭。三股水流喷出潭面，其

unearthed from Anyang, Henan Province, character recorded history of Baotu Spring can be traced back to the Shang Dynasty (1600 B.C.-1046 B.C.). Baotu Spring was called *Luo* in ancient times. More than 2600 years ago, chronicles *The Spring and Autumn Period* recorded "Duke Huan of Lu meets Qi Marquis in *Luo*". When the proser Zeng Gong in the Song Dynasty assumed the governor of Qi Prefecture, he built Luoyuan Hall near the spring and gave *Luoshui* the name Baotu Spring. *Baotu*, is namely

状如玉盘堆雪，声若隐雷，昼夜喷涌，水盛时高达数尺。“趵突”之势自古以来多有记载和颂扬。金代诗人元好问描绘趵突泉为“且向波间看玉塔”。元代著名书画家、诗人赵孟頫在《趵突泉》诗中赞道：“泺水发源天下无，平地涌出白玉壶。”清代文学家蒲松龄则认为趵突泉是“海内之名泉第一，齐门之胜地无双”。

the meaning of spouting, jumping and running, reflecting characteristics of three holes of Baotu Spring bursting and spurting out. Not only is the literal meaning of *Baotu* of classic elegance, but also gives consideration to both sound and meaning, i.e. take *Baotu* to describe the form of water's spouting, jumping, bursting and spurting, and take *Baotu* to imitate the sound when spurting.

Baotu Spring water pours out from three caves, gathering together into a deep pool. Three streams roll out of the surface of the pool; its form is like a pile of snow on the jade plate, and the sound likes hidden thunder. In its prime, it is up to several *Chi* (one third of a meter). Baotu power has many records and high praise since ancient times. The Jin Dynasty poet Yuan Haowen portrayed Baotu Spring, "Just to see jade pagoda among waves." In the Yuan Dynasty, famous painter, poet Zhao Mengfu praised in his poem *Baotu Spring*, "*Luo* water source has no second one in the world; white jade pot is welled out from level ground." Novelist Pu Songling in the Qing Dynasty considered Baotu Spring to be, "The No.1 famous spring throughout the country and famous scenic spot of Qi (a state in the Zhou Dynasty,

趵突泉水最大涌量可达24万立方米/日。泉水清澈见底，清醇甘洌，含菌量极低，是理想的天然饮用水，可以直接饮用。泉水温度一年四季恒定在18℃左右，严冬时节水面上水汽袅袅，像一层薄薄的烟雾，被当地人称为“云蒸雾润”。

now in Shandong) is matchless."

The maximum surge capacity of Baotu Spring is up to 240,000 cubic meters per day.The spring water is so clear that you can see the bottom. It is clean, pure, sweet and crystal-clear; bacteria content is extremely low. It is an ideal natural drinking water, so you can drink directly. All the year round, spring water is constant at about 18℃. In severe winter, the steam is slender and delicate on the surface of the water, like a thin layer of smog, called by the local as "Moistening Steam Fog". Baotu Soar is the first of Jinan Eight Sceneries in the period of the Ming and Qing dynasties.

Places of historic interest and scenic beauty around Baotu Spring are countless.Luoyuan Hall is on the north, which began to be built in the Song Dynasty and was rebuilt in the Qing Dynasty, and the antithetical couplet written by Zhao Mengfu is

泺源堂（图片提供：全景正片）
Luoyuan Hall

“趵突腾空”为明清时期济南八景之首。

趵突泉周边的名胜古迹数不胜数。北有泺源堂，始建于宋代，清代时重建，堂前抱厦柱上刻有元代赵孟頫所撰的对联：“云雾润蒸华不注，波涛声震大明湖。”后院墙壁上有明清以来咏泉诗若干。南为半壁廊水榭。西南有明代所建的观澜亭，中立刻有“趵突泉”“观澜”“第一泉”等文字的明清石碑。泉东为来鹤桥，桥东大片散泉亦汇注成池。如今的趵突泉及附近的古迹群被辟为趵突泉公园，与千佛山、大明湖并称济南三大名胜。

carved on the porch posts in front of the hall, "Mist wave steam rising on Baotu Spring can fill the air dimly discernible to Huafuzhu Mountain in the north of Jinan; surging waves of sound can also be heard in Daming Lake." A few stone inscriptions praising spring since the Ming and Qing dynasties are engraved in backyard walls. On the south, there is half wall's corridor waterside pavilion; on the southwest, there is a Guanlan Pavilion (a pavilion visiting waves) built in the Ming Dynasty, and in the middle stand stelaes of the Ming and Qing dynasties with the words, e.g. "Baotu Spring", "Guanlan" and "The No.1 Spring", etc. On the east of the spring pool is Laihe (Crane Arriving) Bridge; a vast expanse of scattered springs on the east of the bridge also flows together into pool. The present Baotu Spring and nearby monuments group are turned into the Baotu Spring Park, which is equally called "Three Big Scenic Spots of Jinan" together with Qianfo Mountain and Daming Lake.

> 崂山泉

崂山为中国的一座名山，耸立于山东省青岛市东北的黄海之滨。崂山多泉，泉水清澈甘冽。崂山泉中著名的有神水泉、金液泉、天液泉。神水泉位于崂山太清宫三清殿前，一泓碧水，清澈晶莹，旱不枯，雨不溢，水位稳定。相传其为道教神仙太上老君诞生之日，由九龙喷吐的圣洁神水形成，故而得名。金液泉在华楼峰碧落岩上。翠屏岩上的天液泉，相传是天上神仙送到人间的玉液琼浆。

其实崂山泉水并非神龙和仙家所赐，而是大自然作用下形成的天然矿泉。崂山大约形成于7000万年前，频繁的地质构造活动和强烈的岩浆活动，使组成崂山的花岗岩的岩体断裂严重。这为大气降水渗入

> Laoshan Springs

Laoshan Mountain is a famous mountain in China, standing in the northeast beach of the Yellow Sea in Qingdao City, Shandong Province. Laoshan Mountain has many springs; the spring water is clear, sweet and chill. The famous ones in Laoshan springs are Shenshui (god water) Spring, Jinye (holy liquid) Spring and Tianye (heaven liquid) Spring, etc. Shenshui Spring is located in front of Sanqing Hall of Taiqing Temple. Deep and broad blue water is clear glittering and translucent. It is not dry during drought years, and it is not overflow during rainy years; the water level is stable. According to legend, it was formed by holy water spitting by nine dragons on the birthday of the Taoist immortal Lord Laozi, hence came the name. Jinye Spring is on Biluo Rock of Hualou Peak. Tianye Spring

• 崂山风光（图片提供：全景正片）
Scenery of Laoshan Mountain

花岗岩成为地下水创造了有利条件。地下水沿裂隙等流动时，不仅溶入了钾、钠、钙、镁等对人体有益的矿物质，还溶入了花岗岩岩体形成时在高温下分离出来的、留存于岩石裂隙中的大量二氧化碳。崂山泉水中的二氧化碳含量极高，是一般泉水的数十倍。因此，当地下水出露地表时，由于压力变小或温度升高，其中所含的大量二氧化碳便会从水中逸出，形成气泡。

崂山泉水喝到口中清凉舒爽，有醇美之感，故而人们称崂山泉水为“天然汽水”。这种泉水会将人

• 崂山神水泉（图片提供：全景正片）
Shenshui Spring in Laoshan Mountain

is on Cuiping Rock, which according to legend, is the nectar given by the heaven immortals.

In fact, Laoshan Spring water is not granted by magic dragon and immortals, but natural mineral springs formed under the effect of nature. Laoshan formed about 70 million years ago. It was subject to frequent geological tectonic activities, and intense magmatic activities, so that the Laoshan granite rock mass fracture was in a crisscross pattern, which brought about favourable conditions for atmospheric water to permeate granite and become groundwater. Groundwater flows along the fractures, not only minerals beneficial to human body, such as potassium, sodium, calcium, magnesium, etc.,dissolve into the water, but also large amounts of carbon dioxide remaining in rock cracks when separated at high temperature in the rock mass formation dissolve into the water. Laoshan Spring water has a very high carbon dioxide content, which is dozens of times than that of general spring water. Therefore, when the groundwater comes out to ground surface, because the pressure is smaller or the temperature is higher, a large amount of carbon dioxide in it out from the water, forming bubble on the water surface.

- 青岛啤酒
Tsingtao Beer

体内的热量带出，令人感到清爽，故而古时被赋予了“仙饮”之称。崂山泉水用以泡茶，清香可口。崂山泉泡崂山茶，是绝佳的搭配。用以酿酒，不仅酒味醇厚，且口感柔和，香味四溢。著名的青岛啤酒和青岛葡萄酒都是用崂山泉水酿制而成的。

When drinking Laoshan Spring water, you will feel cool and refreshing, so people call Laoshan Spring water "natural soda". Such spring water can bring out heat quantity within the human body, making one feel refreshing. So in ancient times, it was given the name "immortal drink". Make tea with Laoshan Spring water, feeling refreshing and delicious; making Laoshan tea with Laoshan Spring water is the perfect collocation. When used to brew beer and make wine, it is not only mellow, but tastes soft, fragrance overflowing. The famous Tsingtao Beer and Qingdao wine are brewed and made with Laoshan Spring water.

崂山

崂山海拔1132.7米，是中国海岸线上的第一高峰，有“海上第一名山”之称。在崂山方圆几百平方千米内，山海相连，雄山险峡，水秀云奇。古人赞曰：“群峰削玉三千仞，乱石穿空一万丈。”

据说秦始皇、汉武帝皆曾到此寻求仙药。宋元以后人们更是不断修筑上清宫和下清宫等古刹殿宇。这里成为名胜古迹荟萃的宗教名山，也是避暑、游览胜地。著名道教人士丘处机、张三丰等曾在崂山修道，这里至今仍保存着规模宏大、历史悠久的道观太清宫。

崂山除了有名泉、道观之外，还产名茶。相传崂山茶由丘处机、张三丰从江南移植，并亲手培植而成。

• **崂山太清宫**（图片提供：全景正片）

太清宫又名“下清宫”，始建于汉武帝建元元年（前140年），位于崂山南麓老君峰下，是崂山上最大的道观。

Taiqing Temple in Laoshan Mountain

Taiqing Temple is also known as Xiaqing Temple, built in the first year of Jianyuan period of Emperor Wu of the Han Dynasty (140 B.C.). It is located in the south of Laoshan Mountain, below Laojun Peak, being the largest Taoist temple in Laoshan Mountain.

Laoshan Mountain

The height of Laoshan Mountain is 1132.7 meters, which is the first peak along China's coastline, having the name of "The No.1 Famous Mountain on the Sea". Within a radius of several hundred square kilometers of Laoshan Mountain, the mountain connects with the sea. There are grand mountains and dangerous gorges, with beautiful waters and surprising clouds. Ancients praised, "Group of peaks with a height of thousands of meters is like cutting jades. Ruleless giant stones with a height of tens of thousands of meters pierce through clouds."

According to folk legend, the First Emperor of Qin and Emperor Wu of Han formerly sought elixir here. After the Song and Yuan dynasties, ancient Buddhist temples, such as Shangqing Temple and Xiaqing Temple, etc. were unceasingly built, becoming a famous religious mountains gathering together with places of historic interest and scenic beauty, and also a summer tour resort. The famous Taoist personage Qiu Chuji and Zhang Sanfeng, etc. once cultivated themselves according to a religious doctrine in Laoshan. So far, Taoist temple Taiqing Temple has been preserved, which is broad in scale and has a long history.

Laoshan Mountain produces famous tea, besides having famous springs and Taoist temples. According to legend, Qiu Chuji and Zhang Sanfeng transplanted Laoshan tea trees from the South and cultivated personally.

• 崂山茶园（图片提供：全景正片）

Tea Plantation in Laoshan Mountain

> 晋祠三泉

晋祠三泉位于山西省太原市的著名古迹晋祠内。三泉即善利、鱼沼、难老三泉。这三股清泉为晋祠增添了小桥流水的情趣、曲径通幽的意境。这里的泉水发现得很早，《山海经》中载："悬瓮之山，晋水出焉。"唐代大诗人李白曾有诗赞曰"晋祠流水如碧玉"。

据勘查，悬瓮山和山前倾斜平原的疏松盖层下面的基岩面，为地质时代的大断层造成的一个东西向的三级阶梯构造的承压盆地。其中中间的台阶由于受两侧断层的影响，所受挤压作用最强，造成张裂隙发育。这些裂隙又受地下水的侵蚀、溶解，经年累月，不断扩大形成溶洞。悬瓮山石灰岩中的地下水，就是从中

> Three Springs in Jinci Temple

Three Springs in Jinci Temple is located in the famous historic site Jinci Temple, Taiyuan City, Shanxi Province. Three springs are Shanli (kind benefit) Spring, Yuzhao (natural fish pond) Spring and Nanlao (never aging) Spring. The three springs add tastes of water flowing beneath a little bridge and the prospect of a winding path leading to a secluded spot to Jin Memorial Temple. The spring here is found very early. *Guideways of Mountains and Seas* says, "Jinshui River flows from Xuanweng Mountain (Hanging Jar Mountain)." Poet Li Bai in the Tang Dynasty praises in his poem, "Flowing water near Jinci Temple is like jasper."

According to the survey, the surface of the bedrock under the Xuanweng

• **晋祠善利泉亭**

善利泉亭建于善利泉上，为八角攒尖式，与难老泉亭南北对峙，立于圣母殿左右翼。“善利”典出《老子》：“上善若水，水善利万物而不争。”

Shanli Spring Pavilion in Jinci Temple

Shanli Spring Pavilion is built on Shanli Spring with a type of octagonal pavilion roof, which stands facing each other north-south with Nanlao Spring Pavilion on the left and right sides of the Saint Mother's Hall. *Shanli* comes from the allusion *Laozi*, "Highest excellence is like that of water, which benefits all things on earth but do not struggle for the fame and fortune."

间台阶的溶洞中涌出，并冲破松散的堆积层而形成的。

晋祠泉水的水源主要来自汾河河水和大气降水。尽管不同的水源在水质、水温等方面都有较大的不同，但经过长时间和长距离的渗流、混合、滞留与调节，泉水的性

Mountain and the loosen cover layer of the sloping plain in front of the mountain, which is the large fault during the geologic period creating pressure-bearing basin of east-west three-level ladder. Due to the influence of fault on two sides, the intermediate step receives the strongest squeeze effect causing open cracks

晋祠

晋祠位于山西省太原市西南郊25千米处的悬瓮山麓。据《史记》记载，周武王幼子叔虞被封于唐地（今山西太原一带），称唐叔虞。叔虞的儿子燮（xiè），因境内有晋水，改国号为“晋”。后人为了奉祀叔虞，在晋水源头建立了祠宇，称“唐叔虞祠”，即晋祠。

晋祠素以雄伟的建筑群、高超的塑像艺术闻名于世。这里集中国古代祭祀建筑、园林、雕塑、壁画、碑刻艺术等珍贵的历史文化遗产为一体，是世界建筑、园林、雕刻艺术中心。多少年来一直有“不游晋祠，枉到太原”之说。

晋祠有三绝：一是周柏、隋槐，即北周时种植的柏树和隋代时种植的槐树，至今仍生机勃勃、郁郁苍苍；二是圣母殿内的宋代彩塑，它们是中国雕塑史上的精品；三是晋祠三泉之一的难老泉。

• 晋祠十方奉圣禅寺
Fengsheng Temple

Jinci Temple

Jin Memorial Temple is located in the foothill of Xuanweng Mountain, 25km from southwest suburb of Taiyuan in Shanxi Province. According to the *Historical Records*, the youngest son Shuyu of King Wu of Zhou was conferred Tangdi (now Taiyuan, Shanxi Province) upon, then called Tang Shuyu. The son of Shuyu, Xie, because the territory had Jinshui Riven, changed the name of the country for Jin. Dedicated to Shuyu, the posterity set up the ancestral temple in the source of Jinshui River, known as "Tang Shuyu Memorial Temple", i.e. Jinci Temple.

Jinci Temple is famous in the world for its magnificent buildings and superb statue art. Here is the collection of precious historical and cultural heritage as a whole, such as ancient Chinese architectures for sacrifice, gardens, statues, murals and art of inscriptions on a tablet. It is the world art center of architectures, gardens and statues. For many years, there has been a saying, "Not to tour Jinci Temple means arriving at Taiyuan City in vain."

Jinci Temple has three wonders. The first is the Zhou cypress and the Sui locust tree, i.e. cypress planted in the North Zhou and locust tree planted in the Sui Dynasty. Up to now, they have still been full of vigour and heavy blackish green. The second is the figures of maidervants in the Song Dynasty within the Saint Mother's Hall, which are masterpieces in the Chinese statue history. The third is Nanlao Spring (the Never Aging Spring), which is one of the three springs in Jinic Temple.

• 晋祠圣母殿内的宋代侍女彩塑

Figures of Maidservents in the Song Dynasty within the Saint Mother's Hall in Jinci Temple

质趋于稳定，不因季节性气候的变化而变化。晋祠泉的涌水量四季稳定，水质经久不变，清澈晶莹。

晋祠三泉中以难老泉的出水量最大。其为晋水的源头，千年不停，昼夜不息。早在战国时代，晋

• **太原晋祠难老泉亭**

北齐天保年间，在难老泉上建难老泉亭，亭上建水母楼，供奉"水母"。难老泉名取自《诗经·鲁颂》中的"永锡难老"。

Nanlao Spring Pavilion in Jinci Temple, Taiyuan

During the Tianbao period of Norther Qi, Nanlao Spring Pavilion was built above the Nanlao Spring. Shuimu Temple was built on the pavilion, consecrating Shuimu (water god). The name of Nanlao Spring was taken from the brilliant sentence "*Yongxi Nanlao* (never aging)" in *The Book of Songs • Ode to Lu.*

growth. These fissures are corroded and dissolved by groundwater, month after month and year after year, down to continue expanding to form a cave. The groundwater in limestone of Xuanweng Mountain just pours out from the middle step cave and breaks through inattentive accumulation layer to form springs.

The spring water source of Jinci Temple is mainly from Fenhe River and atmospheric water. Although different sources of water have superior differences in water quality and water temperature, after a long time and long distance transfusion, mixing, retention and regulation, the nature of the spring tends to be stable, not varying with seasonal climate change. Water yield of springs of Jinci Temple is stable all the year round. The water quality is everlasting, clear, glittering and translucent.

Among the three springs in Jinci Temple, the water yield of Nanlao Spring is the largest, which is the water source of Jinshui River, no break during the millennium and never ceasing day and night. Early in the Warring States Period, ditches were built in front of the Jinci Temple, using spring water to irrigate farmlands. Fan Zhongyan in the Song Dynasty formerly praised, "Thousands

祠前便已修建沟渠，用泉水灌溉田地。宋代范仲淹曾赞曰：“千家溉禾稻，满目江乡田……皆如晋祠下，生民无旱年。”

families irrigate millet and rice fields all that in my eyes··· If all land like that near the Jinci Temple, creatures would have no drought years."

• 晋祠水母楼
Shuimu Temple

> 中泠泉

中泠泉位于江苏省镇江市金山之西约半千米处的石弹山下，也称“中濡泉”“中零泉”。这是因其原在长江之中，为江水中的一股甘泉，故而得名。泉水绿如翡翠，浓似琼浆。

当年中泠泉只有在枯水季节，长江水位下降时，泉眼才能露出水面。当时汲取泉水十分不易，需在子时或者午时（午夜或正午十二点），用一种特制的器具——盖子十分严紧的铜瓶或铜葫芦，以绳子系住瓶盖，下放至泉眼处，在水下打开盖子，才能汲到真正的泉水。

中泠泉泉水甘冽醇厚，特宜煎茶，有“盈杯不溢”之说。就是将泉水贮于杯中，水即使高出杯口也不会外溢，水面放上一枚硬币，不

> Zhongling Spring

Zhongling Spring is located at the foot of Shidan Mountain which is about half a kilometer from the west of Jinshan Mountain, Zhenjiang City, Jiangsu Province, also known as Zhongru Spring or Zhongling Spring. This is because it is original in the Yangtze River, a sweet spring in the river, hence the name. The spring water is green as jadite and thick as nectar.

In those years, only during low-water seasons, the water level of Yangtze River declined, and the mouth of the Zhongling Spring can be shown out of the water surface. At that time, it is not easy to derive the spring water; it is necessary, at *Zishi* (the period of the day from 11 p.m. to 1 a.m.) or *Wushi* (the period of the day from 11 a.m. to 1 p.m.), to use a tailor-made utensil—copper bottle or copper gourd with tight cover, to tie the cap with

金山

金山位于镇江市西北，古时是长江中的一座岛屿，有“江心一朵美芙蓉”之称。相传唐代时住在山上的僧人裴头陀在江边挖土时挖出一批黄金，并将其献给皇帝。皇帝下令将黄金交还裴头陀，让他在此创建寺庙，并赐名“金山寺”，山也因寺而得名。

金山海拔44米，山上寺院相衔，楼塔争辉，远远望去只见寺塔不见山，故有“金山寺裹山”的说法。

Jinshan Mountain (Gold Mountain)

Jinshan Mountain is located in the northwest of Zhenjiang City. In ancient times, it is an island in the center of Yangtze River, with a name of "a beautiful hibiscus in the middle of the river ". According to legend, in the Tang Dynasty, the monk Pei Toutuo living in the mountain dug out a batch of gold during his earth cutting on riverside, and consecrated them to the emperor. The emperor ordered to pay the gold back to Pei Toutuo to create a temple, and issued imperial order "Jinshan Temple", and the mountain was also named after the temple.

Jinshan Mountain is 44 meters above sea level. Temples connected one by one on the mountain. Looking out far and away, you can see only the Buddhist pagoda not the hill, so there is the saying, "The Jinshan Temple binding the mountain."

• 金山寺（图片提供：全景正片）
Jinshan Temple

会沉底。相传，唐代宗时，湖州刺史李季卿在镇江遇到“茶圣”陆羽，即命人携带铜瓶驾舟到江中汲取泉水，并请陆羽品评。陆羽刚呷了一小口，便说此水并非中泠泉泉水。取水者大为叹服。原来在取水过程中，船遇到风浪，铜瓶里的水洒了一些，取水者贪图省事便以江水补足。南宋名将文天祥（1236—1283）路过此泉，并赋诗为记，首句即为“扬子江心第一泉”。出于对名将的崇拜，世人多接受文天祥的评定，认为中泠泉为“天下第一泉”。

沧海桑田，原来的江中孤岛金山在清代咸丰、同治年间与长江南岸连接起来，中泠泉才最终成为陆地泉。中泠泉成为陆地泉之后，曾一度消失，后于同治八年（1869年）被人发现，在泉眼四周垒石为池，并在此立碑、建亭，池旁构筑亭榭。后来又开拓池数十亩，开塘种植荷芰，又筑土堤，种柳万株，以抵挡江流冲击。池南建有一座八角亭，取名“鉴亭”。

a rope, put it down to the depth of the mouth of the spring, open the cap under the water and you can draw real spring water.

Zhongling Spring water is sweet, crystal-clear and mellow, especially suitable to brew tea. There is the saying, "The most full cup does not overflow." Exactly, store spring water in the cup, it will not overflow though the water is a little higher than the rim of a cup; put a coin on the water surface, it will not sink to the bottom. According to legend, during the reign of Emperor Daizong in the Tang Dynasty, Huzhou *Cishi* (provincial governor) Li Jiqing met the "Tea Sage" Lu Yu in Zhenjiang. He ordered people carrying copper bottle and sailed to draw spring water in the river, and requested Lu Yu to judge. Lu Yu just took a sip of water, and said that was not Zhongling Spring water. The water intake man was captured. Actually, in the intake process, the ship encountered stormy waves, so water in the copper bottle sprinkled some; the man,eager to save trouble, made up for it with water from the river. In the Southern Song Dynasty, the famous general Wen Tianxiang (1236-1283) passed by the spring, and composed a poem to record,

文天祥像
Portrait of Wen Tianxiang

and the first sentence is "the first spring of the Yangtze River". For the worship of the famous general, common people accept Wen Tianxiang's assessment; they consider Zhongling spring as "The First Spring in the World".

Time bringing great changes to the world, during the reign of Emperor Xianfeng and Emperor Tongzhi in the Qing Dynasty, the original islet in the river, Jinshan Mountain linked up with the south bank of the Yangtze River. Zhongling Spring eventually became a land spring. After that, it was once lost; later in the 8th year during the reign of Emperor Tongzhi (1869), it was found. People stacked stones all around the spring to form the pool, and then set up a tablet, built a pavilion and built the hall and pavilion on terrace by the pool. Then people expanded the area of pool to tens of acres, dug ponds to plant lotus, built banks of earth, and planted the of thousands of willows to resist the impact of river flow. An octagonal pavilion was built on the south of the pool, named Jianting Pavilion.

• 池南面石栏上的“天下第一泉”五个大字和池南的鉴亭（图片提供：全景正片）

Characters "The First Spring in the World" on Stone Fence in the South of the Pool, and Jianting Pavilion on the South of the Pool

> 惠山泉

惠山泉位于江苏省无锡市西郊惠山山麓，泉因山而得名。惠山海拔328米，有九个山峰，如同九条苍龙，加上惠山多清泉，历史上有“九龙十三泉”之说。

惠山泉为其中的名泉，原名“漪澜泉”，在惠山第一峰白石坞之下，分上、中、下三池。上池为八角形，水质最优；中池为方形，相传是唐朝大历元年至十二年（766—777）开凿的；下池为方形，水面最大，系宋代所凿，虽与上池一脉相通，但水质不如上池清澈。水质优良的上池水，被陆羽在《茶经》中排列为“第二泉”，自此之后惠山泉便成了公认的“天下第二泉”。惠山泉泉水无色透明，含矿物质少，水质优良，甘美适

> Huishan Spring

Huishan Spring is located at the foot of Huishan Mountain in the western suburbs of Wuxi City, Jiangsu Province. The spring was named after the mountain. Huishan Mountain is 328 meters above sea level, with nine peaks, like nine black dragon, together with many clear springs in Huishan Mountain. In history, thus, there was a saying of the "nine dragons and thirteen springs".

Huishan Spring is a famous spring among them. Its primitive name is Yilan Spring (ripple spring), at the foot of Baishiwu, the first peak of Huishan Mountain. And there are three pools (upper, middle and lower). The upper pool is octagonal, with optimum water quality; the middle pool is square, and according to legend, it was dug in the 1st-12th years of Dali period in the Tang Dynasty (766-777); the lower pool

• 惠山泉上池和中池

The Upper Pool and the Middle Pool of Huishan Spring

• **惠山泉下池**
The Lower Pool of Huishan Spring

口。其原因是由于惠山岩石地层为石英砂岩，地下水从地层中涌向地面时，水中杂质多数在渗滤过程中被除去。

相传唐代宰相李德裕酷爱惠山泉水，曾令地方官吏用坛封装，不分昼夜地驰马传递数千里送至长安（今陕西西安），供他煎茶。宋朝时，惠山泉泉水的声誉更高，宋徽宗时一度成为进献宫廷的贡品。明朝时，惠山泉更成了文人墨客品

is square, with the largest surface of the water, which was dug in the Song Dynasty. Although it is intimately tied up with the upper pool, water quality is not as clear as it. High quality upper pool's water was ranked "The Second Spring" by Lu Yu in *Tea Classics*. Since then, Huishan Spring became recognized as "*The Second Spring in the World*". Huishan Spring water is colorless and transparent, containing less minerals; the water quality is good, sweet and

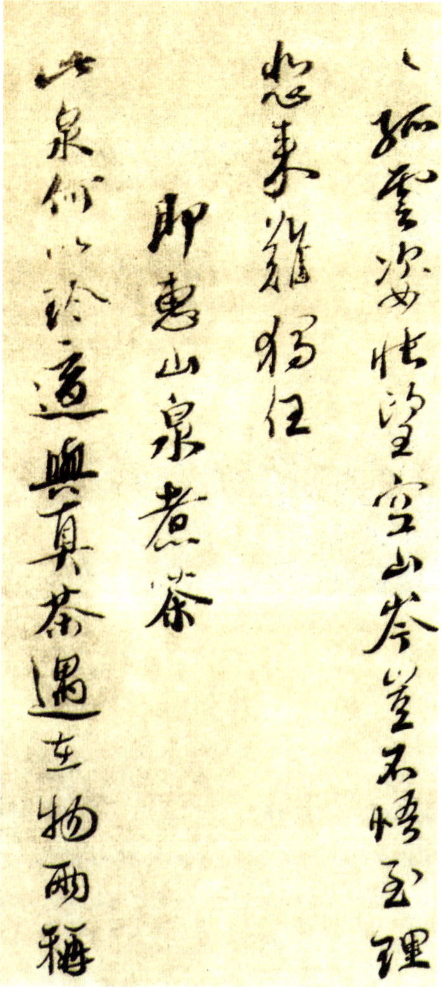

• 《即惠山泉煮茶》【局部】蔡襄（北宋）

蔡襄（1012—1067），北宋书法家，茶学专家。他在《即惠山泉煮茶》中描写了品茶品泉之道。

Reaching Huishan Spring to Brew Tea [Part], by Cai Xiang (Northern Song Dynasty, 960-1127)

Cai Xiang (1012-1067), is a calligrapher and tea expert in the Northern Song Dynasty. He described the method of tasting tea and spring water in his *Reaching Huishan Spring to Brew Tea*.

palatable. The reason is that Huishan Mountain lithostratigraphy is quartz sandstone; when groundwater pours out from the stratum to the earth's surface, most impurities in the water are removed in the percolation and filtration process.

According to legend, Prime Minister Li Deyu in the Tang Dynasty ardently loved Huishan Spring. He formerly ordered local officials to use jars to carry Huishan Spring water and ride thousands of miles without day and night to send water to Chang'an (now Xi'an, Shaanxi Province) for him to brew tea. In the Song Dynasty, Huishan Spring water had an excellent reputation. In the reign of the Emperor Huizong in the Song Dynasty, it once became an aulic presented tribute. In the Ming Dynasty, Huishan Spring further became the place for men of literature and writing to sample tea, play and ceaselessly write poems. The famous painter Wen Zhengming, on February 19th, Tomb-sweeping Day, in the 13th year of Zhengde period in the Ming Dynasty (1518), used tea to entertain friends in Huishan Mountain. They had a whale of a good time and made *Picture of Huishan Tea Party*, reappearing the scene of the poet and the painter brewing tea on the bamboo stove, and thinking at

茗、游玩、题咏的地方。著名画家文徵明，在明正德十三年（1518年）二月十九清明节，与友人茶会于惠山，兴之所至挥毫作了《惠山茶会图》，展现了诗人、画家竹炉煮茗、茅亭随想的情景。清朝康熙皇帝和乾隆皇帝都曾多次到无锡，每次对惠山泉泉水必加品尝和题咏。

由于受到清朝帝王的青睐，地方官着意对惠山泉周围进行整修，建造了池沼、石刻、假山和亭台厅室，配置了花草树木，使其成为一个精致的古典庭院。惠山泉泉水

thatched pavilion. Emperor Kangxi and Emperor Qianlong in the Qing Dynasty formerly went to Wuxi for many times; each time, they must taste Huishan Spring water and write poems to praise something.

Because of the favor of emperors in the Qing Dynasty, local officials deliberately renovated Huishan Spring surroundings; they dug ponds and laid carved stones, rockeries, pavilions and rooms, and configured flowers and trees, making it a fine classical garden. Huishan Spring water flows out from the hornless dragon head carved on the spring wall; The water makes tinkling sound. Erquan

• 《惠山茶会图》 文徵明（明）
Picture of Tea Party in Huishan Mountain, Wen Zhengming (Ming Dynasty, 1368-1644)

• “天下第二泉”
Characters "The Second Spring in the World" on the stone

自泉壁石雕的螭首中流出，叮咚作响，清脆悦耳。泉畔建有二泉亭，泉池旁的大石上，镌刻着元代著名书法家赵孟頫所题的“天下第二泉”五个大字。

Pavilion is built beside the spring. Five big characters "The Second Spring in the World" are engraved on the large stone beside the spring, which is inscribed by the famous calligrapher Zhao Mengfu in the Yuan Dynasty.

惠山泥人

惠山泥人是无锡著名特产，是由当地艺人取惠山特有的黑泥捏塑而成的。这种黑泥质地细腻柔软，有弹性，不易断裂，因而具有极佳的可塑性。

惠山泥人始创于1000多年前的南北朝时期，在明代时发展到鼎盛。后来因昆曲的流行，出现了许多以戏曲人物为题材的手捏戏文人物。20世纪30年代，惠山泥人工艺融入石膏制作的技法，产生了石膏工艺泥人的新品种。惠山泥人工艺也逐渐形成了富有地方特色的“惠山型”风格泥塑工艺。

惠山泥人的制作工艺分为捏坯、彩绘和开相几部分。其中彩绘在整个制作过程中占有较高的比重，有“三分塑七分彩”之说。常用的色彩是红、绿、黄、青等颜色，具有鲜明亮丽的特点。惠山泥人中的代表作品是“大阿福”，它是一个健壮可爱的孩子形象，具有镇邪、降福之意。

Huishan Clay Figurines

Huishan clay figurines are famous specialty of Wuxi. Local artists knead models by taking the typical black clay of Huishan Mountain. Such black mud has exquisite and soft quality, being resilient and not easy to break, so it has excellent plasticity.

Huishan clay figurines were founded more than 1000 years ago in the Northern and Southern dynasties. In the Ming Dynasty, it developed to its heyday. And later as a result of the prevalence of Kunqu Opera, there were many handmade clay figurines taking opera characters as the subject matter. In the 1930s, Huishan clay figurines technology learned from gypsum production techniques, producing new varieties of the plaster craft clay figurines. The craft of Huishan clay figurine has gradually featured a distinctive local characteristic.

Huishan clay figurines' making process is divided into several parts, i.e. parison kneading, color decoration and painting the eyes; wherein color decoration has a higher proportion in the entire production process; there is the saying "three-tenth of modeling and seven-tenth of coloring". Common used colors are red, green, yellow and blue, etc., having the bright and glamorous characteristics. The representative work of Huishan clay figurines is *Da'afu*, which looks like a robust and lovely child, to be blessed and ward off evils hopefully.

• 惠山泥人“大阿福”
Huishan Clay Figurines, *Da'afu*

> 观音泉

观音泉位于江苏省苏州市虎丘观音殿后，泉井井口约3.4平方米，围以石壁。虎丘是一座小山，位于苏州城西北郊。虎丘历史悠久，景色秀美，享有“吴中第一名胜”的美誉。

据《苏州府志》记载，唐代贞元年间，陆羽曾长期寓居虎丘，一边潜心

> Guanyin Spring

Guanyin Spring is located behind the Guanyin Hall in Huqiu, Suzhou City, Jiangsu Province. The mouth of the spring well is about 3.4 square meters, enclosed by a stone wall. Huqiu is a small hill, located in northwest suburbs of Suzhou City. Huqiu has a long history and beautiful scenery, enjoying the reputation of "The First Scenic Spot in Wuzhong (Now, Suzhou)".

According to *Annals of Suzhou Prefecture*, during the Zhenyuan period in the Tang Dynasty, Lu Yu had a long-term resident in Huqiu. He wrote books with concentration. At the same time, he studied the relations between tea and the water used. He found the Huqiu Spring water is clear, sweet and luscious, so he

• 虎丘风光
Scenery of Huqiu

著书，一边研究茶叶及泡茶所用之水。他发觉虎丘泉水清冽甘美，便在虎丘山上挖掘了一口泉井。所以人们也称观音泉为“陆羽井”。观音泉泉水清澈透明，如碧液琼浆，呷一口微有甜味，用来煎茶能充分展现茶叶的品质。唐代刘伯刍评此水为天下第三，后被世人广泛接受，故此泉又有“第三泉”之称。

dug a spring well in Huqiu. So Guanyin Spring is also referred to as "Well of Lu Yu". Its water is clear and transparent, sipped it with slightly sweet; using it to brew tea can fully reflect the quality of tea. Liu Bochu of the Tang Dynasty ranked the water as the third in the world. After that, it is recognized by the public, and this spring has the name "The Third Spring".

• **观音泉所在的院门**

泉井所在的院门上刻有“第三泉”三个大字。

Courtyard Gate of Guanyin Spring

Three big characters of "The Third Spring" are inscribed on the courtyard gate of Guanyin Spring.

剑池泉、憨憨泉

苏州气候温湿多雨，地下水丰富，花岗岩的过滤作用显著，除了观音泉外，还有诸多良泉。

在虎丘山下与观音泉相通的还有剑池泉。据文献记载，剑池之下为春秋时期（前770—前476）吴国国君阖闾之墓。为建该墓，当时征调10万民夫，凿池三年方成。因阖闾爱剑，下葬时以宝剑三千殉葬。相传秦始皇嬴政和三国时期（220—280）吴国皇帝孙权都曾遣人在此凿石求剑，但皆无功而返。然而凿石处却形成了一个深两丈余的长方形池子，故名为“剑池”。池旁刻有“风壑云泉”四个字，笔法圆润，相传为宋代书法家米芾所书。

在虎丘上山路的西侧，还有一口历史悠久的泉井——憨憨泉。泉井栏圈上和井后壁上都刻有“憨憨泉”三个字，为宋代大书法家吕升卿所书。憨憨泉的名称来历有诸多说法：一说其泉水使一名叫憨憨的失明儿童双眼复明，一说其由梁代（502—557）高僧憨憨寻得。据说其泉眼通海，泉水四季不涸，又名“海涌泉”。

• 虎丘剑池
Jianchi Spring in Huqiu

Jianchi (Sword Pool) Spring and Climate in Suzhou Spring

Climate in Suzhou is warm, wet and rainy, with rich groundwater, and the granite filtering action is notable. In addition to Guanyin Spring, there are still many good springs.

At the foot of Huqiu, there is Jianchi Spring interlinked with Guanyin Spring. According to historical records, under Jianchi was Helv's Tomb, the King of Wu in the Spring and Autumn period (770 B.C.-476 B.C.). For the construction of the tomb then, 100 thousand civilians were called up, chiselling the pond for three years to accomplish it. Because Helv loved swords, three thousand swords were buried when interred. According to legend, the First Emperor of Qin, Ying Zheng and Sun Quan, the emperor of Wu, in the Three Kingdoms period (220-280) both sent people here to chisel stone to seek swords, but they all failed. However, a rectangular pool with the depth of more than 6 meters was formed here. So it was named "*Sword Pool*". The wall besides the pool is engraved with four characters "*Feng He Yun Quan*" (wind gully and cloud spring). The writing is round and smooth. which according to legend, were written by the calligrapher Mi Fu in the Song Dynasty.

On the west side of the road going up Huqiu, there is a long history spring well-Hanhan Spring. Characters "*Hanhan* spring" are engraved on the bar circle and the back wall of spring well, written by the great calligrapher Lv Shengqing in the Song Dynasty. About the origin of the name, there are many stories: one is that its spring water makes a blind child named Hanhan regain eyesight; one is that eminent monk Hanhan in the Liang Dynasty (502-557) found the spring. It is said that the spring connects to the sea, so the spring water does not dry up at all seasons, also known as "*Haiyong Quan* (sea gushing spring)".

• 憨憨泉泉井
Hanhan Spring Well

> 虎跑泉

虎跑泉位于浙江省杭州市西南虎跑山虎跑寺内。杭州民谚中有"龙井茶叶虎跑泉"之说，将龙井茶和虎跑泉并称为"西湖双绝"。用虎跑泉泉水冲泡的龙井茶，清香四溢，被称为"龙虎斗"，是一种上等饮品。

相传，唐元和十四年（819年）曾有高僧在此居住，但苦于山中无水。一夜他梦见一位神仙告诉他说："南岳童子泉，当遣二虎移来。"第二天，果然看见两只猛虎刨地，一股泉水涌出，故名"虎跑泉"。

虎跑泉附近的岩层属于石英砂岩，裂隙较多，透水性能好且岩层向东南倾斜45度。虎跑泉位于砂岩层倾斜的下方，正好吸收岩层面向

> Hupao Spring

Hupao Spring is located in the Hupao Temple, at the foot of Hupao Mountain on the southwest of Hangzhou City, Zhejiang Province. There is a folk saying in Hangzhou, "Longjing tea brewed with Hupao Spring." Longjing tea and Hupao Spring are called "Two Uniqueness of West Lake". Brewing Longjing tea with Hupao Spring water, delicate fragrance overflowing, is known as *Longhudou* (dragon against tiger); it is a superior drink.

According to legend, in the 14th year of Yuanhe period in the Tang Dynasty (819), there once lived an eminent monk, suffering from no water in the mountain. One night he dreamed that an immortal told him: "There is a spring in Hengshan Mountain named Tongzi Spring. I will send two tigers to move it here." The next day, he really saw two tigers digging

虎跑泉眼

The Mouth of Hupao Spring

下渗流的地下水。地下水从难溶解的石英砂岩中渗出，经岩层过滤，渗流至山下，因而水质相当纯净。虎跑泉泉水内的矿物质含量只有20—150毫克/升，比一般泉水要低，这就是其沁人心脾、甘冽甜美的原因。杭州地区湿润多雨，虎跑泉又地处洼地，故而虎跑泉的出水量很大，每昼夜能出190余吨。

the ground, and a stream of spring water poured out, so named Hupao Spring (*hu* means tiger and *pao* means dig in Chinese).

The rock stratum near Hupao Spring belongs to quartz sandstone. With more cracks, water permeability is good and the rock stratum tilts to southeast at an angle of 45°. Hupao Spring is below the inclined sandstone layer so that it can the

• **“虎跑梦泉”石雕**（图片提供：全景正片）

虎跑泉池东南隅的沟谷中，西湖新十景之一的“虎跑梦泉”浮雕真实地再现了“虎移泉眼”的神话故事。在泉池旁还竖立着由斑斓猛虎和倚石而卧的僧人组成的“虎跑梦泉”石雕。

Stone Carving, "*Hupao Mengquan*"

In the cleugh southeast of Hupao Spring, *Hupao Mengquan* is one of the New Ten Scenes of West Lake, which represents the fairy tale of "*Tiger Digging Spring*". By the spring, there is a stone carving, "*named* Hupao Mengguan", composed of gorgeous fierce tigers and a lying monk leaning against a rock.

• 虎跑公园内汲水的市民

there is are Citizen Drawing Water in Hupao Park

vadose groundwater downward along the rock stratum surface. Groundwater oozes out of quartz sandstone difficult to dissolve, and is filtered through the rock stratum, transfusing down the mountain, so the water quality is pure. The mineral substance content of Hupao Spring water is only 20-150 mg/L, lower than general spring water; this is why it is clear and sweet. Hangzhou is humid and rainy, and Hupao Spring is located in the low-lying land, so the water yield of Hupao Spring is large. It can produce 190 tons every day and night.

龙井茶与龙井泉

龙井泉位于浙江省杭州市西湖西南山地中，其西面就是盛产龙井茶的龙井村。这里山色秀丽、泉水淙淙，是西湖外围一处闻名遐迩的风景游览地。

明朝正统十三年（1448年），龙井内曾发现一枚“投龙简”，上刻东吴赤乌年间向“水府龙神”祈雨的告文。可见最晚在三国时期（220—280）龙井泉就已被发现，其闻名于世至少有1700多年了。相传古时每逢干旱，附近的人们都会到此求雨，屡验不爽。人们认为这口井与海相通，其中必有龙，于是便称其为“龙井”。这口泉井四季不干，水味甘甜，清澈如镜。

龙井既是泉名、村名，也是茶名。西湖龙井名扬中外。龙井茶的生长环境得天独厚，加上早期附近寺庙僧侣们的精心培植，终获“中国第一名茶”之称。龙井茶素以“色绿、香郁、味甘、形美”四绝著称于世。龙井茶尤以狮峰山所产的狮峰龙井为上品，声名远播。

用龙井泉水冲泡龙井茶，也是绝佳的组合，历史上有“采取龙井茶，还烹龙井水”之说。

Longjing Tea and Longjing Spring

Longjing Spring is located in the mountainous region on the northwest of West Lake, Hangzhou City, Zhejiang Province. Its west side is Longjing Village rich in Longjing tea. The mountain is delicate and pretty here; the spring water flows with a merry gurgle, which is the well-known sceneic resort of the periphery of the west lake.

In the 13th year of Zhengtong period in the Ming Dynasty (1448), *Toulongjian* (a kind of utensil in Taoism ceremony) was found in Longjing well; a document was engraved on it, praying for rain to the Dragon Deity during the Chiwu period in the state Wu (238-251). It is thus clear that the Longjing Spring was found at latest in the Three Kingdoms period, so it is well known in the world for at least 1700 years. According to legend, in ancient times when it was drought, people nearby would come here to pray for rain; it had been proved effective every time. People thought this well was linked with the sea, and there must be a dragon in it, then people called it *Longjing* (Dragon well). This spring well does not dry out at all seasons, and the water tastes sweet, as clear as a mirror.

Longjing is both the name of the spring, the village, and the name of the tea. West Lake Longjing tea is famous both in China and foreign countries. The growth environment of Longjing tea is richly endowed by nature, coupled with early nearby temple monks' careful cultivation.Thus, it has been awarded the title the "Most Famous Chinese Tea". Longjing Tea is known throughout the world for its four uniqueness: green color, delicate aroma, sweet taste and beautiful shape. Especially, Shifeng Longjing tea produced in Shifeng Mountain is revered as the top one, whose fame spreads far and wide.

Brewing Longjing tea with Longjing Spring water is also the perfect combination.There is a saying in history, "Pick Longjing tea-leaves, still use Longjing Spring water."

• 龙井

Longjing Well

> 谷帘泉

谷帘泉位于江西省九江市庐山主峰汉阳峰南面的康王谷中。康王谷中的泉水，被山石阻滞，百缕细水纷纷散落而下，远远望去像亮丽晶莹的珠帘悬挂谷中，故而得名。庐山为古老变质岩断块山，当地植被繁茂。水通过植被再沿岩石节理向下渗透，最后经过岩层裂隙汇成一泓碧泉，从山涧喷涌而出，倾泻入谷。所以，水质特优。

古人称谷帘泉清、冷、香、柔、甘、净，曾被陆羽评为“天下第一泉”，因而声名远播。历代文人墨客纷然而至，品水留题。北宋学者王禹偁在《谷帘泉序》中描述此泉水为：“其味不败，取茶煮之，浮云散雪之状，与井泉绝殊。”南宋诗人陆游也对谷帘泉称

> Gulian Spring

Gulian Spring is located in Kangwang Valley on south side of Hanyang Peak of the highest peak in Lushan Mountain, Jiujiang City, Jiangxi Province. The spring water in the valley is blocked by mountain rocks. The water flow assumes hundreds of tiny streams scattering to fall down one after another. it looks like a beautiful, bright, sparkling and crystal-clear beaded curtain hanging in the valley from a distance, hence the name. Lushan Mountain consists of ancient metamorphic rocks. The local vegetation is lush, and water goes through the vegetation and seeps downward along the rock joints. Finally it goes through the stratum cracks converging into a blue spring, spurting out from mountain streams and pouring into the valley. Therefore, the water is of extra best quality.

赞不已，在日记中写道："前辈或斥水品以为不可信，水品固不必尽当。然谷帘卓然，非惠山所及，则亦不可诬也。"宋代名士王安石、秦观、朱熹、白玉蟾等都为谷帘泉留下了诸多绚丽的诗篇。

在谷帘泉水流经处的危崖之上，建有一座单层、四角、四柱的观瀑亭，这里是观看谷帘泉的最佳处。为纪念陆羽，后人在亭下修建了鸿渐（陆羽字鸿渐）桥。在康

• 谷帘泉
Gulian Spring

The ancients noted that Gulian Spring has many advantages, i.e. limpidity, coldness, fragrance,softness and cleaning. Gulian Spring is once rated as "The First Spring in the world" by Lu Yu, so its fame spreads far and wide, and it is well-known in the world. The men of literature and writing of past dynasties came in a throng, tasting the water and leaving their comments. The scholar Wang Yucheng in the Northern Song Dynasty described this spring in his *The Preface of Gulian Spring*, "Its taste is unchanged, and the tea shous floating clouds and scattered snow form when brewed with the water of Gulian Spring. It is much more special than well springs." The poet Lu You in the Southern Song Dynasty also said Gulian Spring was beyond praise, and wrote in his diary, "Maybe seniors refute water ranks, which is considered unlikelihood. As water ranks are not necessary to be all suitable, but Gulian Spring's rank is eminent right. Huishan Spring is not as good as Gulian Spring, also criteria cannot be accused falsely." Literary lions in the Song Dynasty-Wang Anshi, Qin Guan, Zhu Xi and Bai Yuchan, etc., all left numerous flowery poems for Gulian Spring.

王城前的山门口，建有一座四柱、三门的牌坊，上书“天下第一泉”五个大字。在山涧岩石之上，多有题刻。在回马石旁的崖壁上，有南宋理学家朱熹用隶书书写的“谷帘泉”三个大字。

庐山云雾茶是庐山的一大名产，也是中国十大名茶之一。庐山云雾茶由于长年受庐山云雾滋润，所产茶芽叶粗壮、白毫显露，喝起来满口生香、浓郁甘醇。谷帘泉

Above precipitous cliffs by which Gulian Spring water flows, a monolayer, quadrangle and four posts waterfall-watching pavilion is built, which is the optimum place to watch Gulian Spring. In commemoration of Lu Yu's, later generations built Hongjian (the style name of Lu Yu) Bridge below the pavilion. At the mountain entrance in front of Kangwang City, a memorial archway of four posts and three gateways, Chinese characters "The First

庐山风光
Scenery of Lushan Mountain

• 庐山云雾茶
Lushan Yunwu Tea

水，云雾名茶，再加上庐山胜景，使得庐山成为古往今来深受人们喜欢的旅游胜地。

Spring in the World" are witten on it. On rocks in mountain creeks, there are many inscriptions. On the precipice near Huima (horse turning) Stone, Chinese characters *Gulian* Sping were written in official script by the Confucian psychology scholar Zhu Xi in the Southern Song Dynasty.

Lushan Yunwu (cloud and mist) tea is a famous product of Lushan Mountain, which is one of China's Top Ten Famous Teas. Because Lushan Mountain's cloud and mist moisten the tea all the year round, the tea buds and leaves are stout, with small and tiny hair. When drunk, it make the mouth full of aroma and tastes mellow. Gulian Spring, Lushan Yunwu tea and wonderful Lushan Mountain scenery make Lushan Mountain a famous place where people like to travel from ancient to modern times.

庐山

庐山地处江西省北部，是世界级名山，1996年被列入《世界遗产名录》。世界遗产委员会给予其极高的评价："江西庐山是中华文明的发扬地之一。这里的佛教和道教庙观，代表理学观念的白鹿洞书院，代表古代高科技建筑的观音桥以其独特的方式融汇在具有突出价值的自然美之中，形成了具有极高的美学价值，与中华民族精神和文化生活紧密联系的文化景观之一。"

相传殷商时，有匡氏兄弟结庐隐居于此，故庐山又称“匡庐”或“匡山”。庐山风景以“雄、奇、险、秀”闻名于世，素有“匡庐奇秀甲天下”的美誉。主峰汉阳峰，海拔1473.4米。庐山四季气候特点为春温、夏凉、秋爽、冬寒。盛夏酷暑季节，庐山却温和如春，因而成为著名的避暑胜地。庐山地区降水丰富，加上砂岩构成的雄伟山体，故多瀑布。最著名的三叠泉分三级飞泻，一级最大落差60米，气势极为雄伟，被誉为“庐山第一景观”。

庐山不仅风光秀丽，还具有无比丰厚的内涵。千百年来，无数文人墨客、名人志士在此留下了脍炙人口的诗篇。苏轼的“不识庐山真面目，只缘身在此山中”描写了庐山云雾缭绕的仙境；李白的“飞流直下三千尺，疑是银河落九天”描绘了庐山瀑布的雄奇壮丽。除了这些自然的风光之外，庐山上还有居中国四大书院之首的白鹿洞书院、唐寅《庐山图》中的观音桥、周瑜鄱阳湖练兵点将之处周瑜点将台等数不胜数的历史古迹。

三叠泉瀑布

The Three-fold Spring Waterfall

Lushan Mountain

Lushan Mountain is located in the northern part of Jiangxi Province; it is a world-renowned mountain. In 1996, Lushan Mountain was appraised by World Heritage Committee of UNESCO as a world cultural landscape and inscribed on the World Heritage List. The committee gave it a high evaluation, "Jiangxi Lushan Mountain is one of the origins of Chinese civilization. The Buddhist and Taoist temples, the White Deer Cave Academy representing Confucian psychology ideas, and the Guanyin Bridge representing the ancient high-tech architecture, blend in their style, and more particularly, their settings with its outstanding natural beauty to create cultural landscape of outstanding aesthetic value, and also powerful associations with Chinese spiritual and cultural life."

It is said that in the Shang Dynasty, there were brothers of the Kuang Family who came to Lushan Mountain to cultivate themselves in order to attain immortality, so it is also called "Kuanglu Mountain" or "Kuangshan Mountain". The scenery of Lushan Mountain earns its fame with its grandiosity, peculiarity, perilousness and elegance. It usually has the reputation of "Kuanglu Mountain's wonderful beauty is peerless in the world". The main peak, Hanyang Peak is 1473.4 meters above sea level. It is warm in spring, cool in summer, bright in autumn and cold in winter; in the deepest summer, it is as mild as spring, thus becoming a famous summer resort. Lushan Mountain area has abundant rainfall, with majestic sandstone mountain body, so there are many waterfalls. The most famous Three-fold Spring flows swiftly in three levels; the maximum drop is 60 meters; the scenery is very magnificent, having the reputation of the "First Marvelous Spectacle of Lushan Mountain".

Lushan Mountain has not only beautiful scenery, but also matchless and rich connotation. For thousands of years, countless men of literature and writing, famous persons and ambitions people left poems winning universal praise. Poet Su Shi's "I can't tell the true face of Lushan Mountain because I am in the mountain" depicts the Lushan Mountain wonderland covered in mist. Poet Li Bai's "Upon seeing the falling waterfalls from the precipice, I couldn't help wondering whether it is the masterpiece of the Milky Way pouring down from heaven" depicts the magnificent scenery of the waterfall on Lushan Mountain. In addition to these natural sceneries, there are still countless historic sites, e.g. the White Deer Cave Academy regarded as the first of China's Top Four Ancient Academies, Guanyin Bridge in Tang Yin's painting *Lushan Mountain* and Zhou Yu Dianjiang (calling the roll of officers) Terrace where Zhou Yu training troops and calling the roll of officers and assigning them tasks in Poyang Lake, etc.

• 白鹿洞书院
The White Deer Cave Academy

> 福州温泉群

福州是中国东南沿海重要都市，也是福建省的省会。福州地区温暖潮湿，降水充沛，雨水不断地沿裂隙下渗形成丰富的地下水。而福州盆地又是岩浆活动强烈的地区，地下水容易向地壳深部渗透，在岩浆热作用的影响下逐渐形成热水，并储存起来。而经过福州的西向断裂带给热水的出露提供了通道，形成了浅层中温热水和温泉出露带。福州温泉出露带的面积约占福州市面积的七分之一，地热储量达9800立方米，形成了福州温泉群。

福州温泉以数量多、水质佳享誉全国，自古便有“福州温泉甲东南”之誉。宋代人编纂的《三山志》中，对福州温泉的出露情况、

> Fuzhou Hot Spring Group

Fuzhou is an important coastal city in the southeast China, and also the capital of Fujian Province. The climate of Fuzhou is warm and humid, with abundant rainfall, and the rainwater constantly infiltrates along the cracks forming abundant groundwater. And Fuzhou basin is a strong magmatic activity area; the groundwater is easy to seep into deep crust, and under the effect of thermal magma, gradually forms hot water savings. Cracks to the west passing Fuzhou provide channels for exposing hot water, forming an exposed zone of shallow hot water in moderated temperature and hot springs. Fuzhou hot springs exposed zone area accounts for about 1/7 of the Fuzhou City, geothermal reserves amounts to 9800 cubic meters, forming Fuzhou hot spring group.

Fuzhou hot springs have the

• **福州风光**（图片提供：全景正片）
Scenery of Fuzhou

特点、水温等作了详细的描述："地多燠泉，数十步必有一穴，或迸河渠中，味甘而性和热，胜者气如硫黄，能熟蹲鸱，旱涝无增减。"据史书记载，福州有名的温

reputation throughout the country in quantity and water quality Therefore, since ancient times, there is a saying that "Fuzhou hot springs are No.1 in the Southeast". Fuzhou hot springs' exposed situation, characteristics and water

泉就有八处之多。到1911年，福州城内有温泉井50—60眼。目前热井已达176眼之多。

早在唐代时，福州人民就发现这里有地下温泉。到北宋嘉祐年间，温泉已被广泛地利用。全盛时期共有大小浴室40多家，并分为“官汤”和“民汤”。

福州的温泉水有助于缓解病痛，主要有三方面的原因：一是温

• 福州温泉公园（图片提供：FOTOE）
Fuzhou Hot Springs Park

temperatures are described in detail in *Three Mountains Annals* compiled by people in the Song Dynasty, "There are many hot springs on the land; there must be one cave within dozens of steps, or spurting into rivers and ditches. The water taste sweet and hot, and the mist of very hot ones emerging like sulfur. It can cook poults. The water level of the spring remains unchanged regardless of drought and flood." According to the historical records, there were as many as eight famous springs; by 1911, there had been 50-60 hot spring wells in Fuzhou; currently hot spring wells already amount to 176.

As early as in the Tang Dynasty, people in Fuzhou found here are underground hot springs. Until the Jiayou period in the Northern Song Dynasty, hot springs had been widely used. In its heyday, there were more than 40 bathrooms big or small, divided into "official hot springs" and "civilian hot springs".

Fuzhou hot spring water contributes to relieving diseases. There are three main reasons. One is the high temperature, generally at 40℃-60℃ and up to the highest 98℃. The second is high water gage, shallow burial; here springs are

• 福州某会馆的温泉泡浴池（图片提供：FOTOE）
Hot Spring Bubble Bath of a Guild Hall in Fuzhou

度高，一般在40℃—60℃，最高可达98℃；二是水压大、埋藏浅，这里的温泉大多深40—65米，涌水量达每秒0.5—1升，钻孔涌水量可达每日900吨，钻孔喷出地表的高度最高可达25.9米；三是水质纯净，无色无味。此外，温泉中还含有钠、钾、氟、氡及少量的钼、镓、钛等元素，对皮肤病、风湿性关节炎、神经痛等治疗有益。

mostly 40-65 meters deep; gushing water yield amounts to 0.5 to 1 liter per second; drilling water yield up to 900 tons per day; the height of water spouting out of the surface from the drilling hole is up to 25.9 m. The third is that the water is pure, colorless and tasteless. In addition, hot springs also contain sodium, potassium, fluorine, radon, molybdenum, gallium, titanium, etc. It can relieve skin diseases, rheumatoid arthritis and neuralgia, etc.

> 从化温泉

从化温泉又称“流溪河温泉”，位于广东省从化市西北。这里气候宜人，四面山峦重叠，环境

> Conghua Hot Spring

Conghua Hot Spring is also called Liuxi (flowing streams) River Spring, located in the northwest of Conghua City, Guangdong Province. The climate

从化风光（图片提供：全景正片）
Scenery of Conghua

幽静，是著名的旅游和疗养胜地。从化温泉从流溪河底涌出，水质好、水温高、泉景佳，被人们称为“岭南第一泉”。

从化温泉发现较早，在明清时期已闻名遐迩。“百丈飞泉”在明

here is pleasant. Mountains range on all sides, and the environment is quite and secluded, which is a famous tourism and health resort. Conghua Hot Spring pours out from the bottom of Liuxi River, having good water quality, high water temperature and beautiful spring scenery,

从化温泉度假村（图片提供：FOTOE）
Hot Spring Resort in Conghua

代时被列为从化县八景之一。清代编纂的《从化县志》中，有该地“其水温热”的记载，但当时尚未开发利用。1931年岭南大学冼玉清教授曾撰文介绍该地区的优美景色和特殊环境。该校化学系的德国医

known as the No.1 spring of *Lingnan* (south of the Five Ridges).

Conghua Hot Spring as a tourist attraction was found earlier, and was well-known far and wide in the Ming and Qing dynasties, *Baizhang Feiquan* was classified as one of the eight sceneries of Conghua County in the Ming Dynasty. In *Conghua County Annals* compiled in the Qing Dynasty, there was the record of "Its water is tepid", but at that time, it was not yet developed and used. In 1931, the professor Xian Yuqing of Lingnan University formerly wrote articles to introduce fine view and special environment of the hot spring. The German doctor Ke Dao of the Chemistry Department in the university analysed the hot spring water and found that it is beneficial to the treatment of multiple diseases, e.g. the skin disease and arthritis, etc. Thereafter Conghua Hot Spring draw the attention of people. Half way up the mountain, there is a huge stone, on which is engraved Tianyi (heaven medicine) Place and this is the evidence of early people using the hot spring. At the open-air in the hot springs area, One can see drizzly white mists with light mist curling up from a distance, and up close, fine stones on the river bottom

温泉药池（图片提供：黎明/FOTOE）

Chemicals Pool of Hot Spring

生柯道对温泉水进行了化验，发现其有益于皮肤病、关节炎等多种疾病的治疗。此后从化温泉渐渐引起人们的注意。在半山腰上有一巨石，上刻有“天医处”，这便是早期人们使用温泉的证据。温泉区的露天泉眼处，远远望去白雾、轻烟袅袅，近看河底细石熠熠发光。泉水从河底石缝中喷涌而出，宛如明镜上滚动着的万斛明珠。

从化温泉的温度一般为59℃，鸡蛋放进去不一会儿就能熟。从化温泉是硅酸泉，又叫苏打泉，比普通水轻软。其无色无味，且含有多种对人体有益的矿物质，如钙、镁、钾、钠、二氧化硅等。从化温泉尤以富含氡气为特色，对于改善人体机能有着积极的作用。

从化温泉之所以闻名，不仅在于它奔涌于明山秀水之间，还在于它有着其他温泉少见的温沙浴。在流溪河的两岸，散布着一堆堆温软的细沙。人们随意在温沙里挖出一个“澡盆”，泉水便从沙底汩汩流出。躺在温沙做成的“澡盆”里，若水过烫，便可从河里放入一些凉水，冷热因人而异，饶有趣味。

are sparkling. The spring water spurts out from rock cracks at the bottom of river, pouring out a chain of boiling beads, like tens of thousands of pearls rolling on a mirror.

The temperature of Conghua Hot Spring is 59℃ generally; eggs are put in and cooked in a moment. Conghua Hot Spring is a silicate spring, also called soda spring, which is more light and soft than ordinary water. And it is colorless and tasteless, containing a variety of minerals beneficial to human body, such as calcium, magnesium, potassium, sodium and silica, etc. Especially, as its characteristic, Conghua Hot Spring is rich in radon, which has a positive effect to the function of the human body.

Conghua Hot Spring is famous, because it not only rushes among beautiful mountains and rivers, but also has thermal sand bathing spa being rare of other hot springs. Along both banks of Liuxi River are interspersed with piles of soft warm fine sands. People can freely dig up a "bathtub" in warm sands; spring water flows out of the sand with a gurgle. Lie in the "bathtub" made of warm sands, if the water is too hot, and just get some cold water in; each takes what he needs, hot or cold. It is most amusing.

> 台湾四大名温泉

台湾省处于亚欧大陆板块的边缘，这里曾发生过频繁的火山喷发。如今这些火山虽已熄灭，不过地下仍有未冷却的火山岩浆，使得这些地区的地热资源丰富，从而形成了台湾众多的温泉。台湾温泉形形色色，有100余处，如同一颗颗璀璨的明珠，镶嵌在富饶美丽的宝岛上，散发着迷人的光彩。其中以北投温泉、阳明山温泉、关子岭温泉和四重溪温泉最为著名，被称为“台湾四大名温泉”。

北投是台湾百年来最著名的“温泉之乡”，位于台北市的最北方，距台北市区约12千米。北投温泉星罗棋布，温泉水质属酸性，含有大量的硫化氢，为硫黄泉，泉温大多在40℃—68℃。温泉区有50

> Top Four Hot Springs in Taiwan

Taiwan Province is in the edge of Eurasian plate; formerly vulcanian eruption frequently happened here. Although nowadays, these volcanos have slept, underground there are still volcano lavas which have not cooled down, making these areas have a large amount of geothermal resources, thereby forming the scene that there are many hot springs in Taiwan Province. Taiwan hot springs are of all forms; the total number is more than 100, like bright pearls inlaid in the rich and beautiful *Baodao* (treasure island), exuding charming splendour. Among them, the Beitou Hot Spring, Yangming Mountain Hot Spring, Guanzi Ridge Hot Spring and Sichong Brook Hot Spring are the most famous, known as the Top Four Hot Springs in Taiwan Province.

• **台湾胜景日月潭**（图片提供：全景正片）

日月潭是台湾最大的天然湖。湖中有一座小岛，远望好像浮在水面上的一颗明珠，名曰光华岛。以此岛为界，北半湖形状似圆日，南半湖形状如弯月，因而得名。

Wonderful Scenery of Sun-Moon Lake, Taiwan Province

Riyuetan Pool in Taiwan Province is the largest natural lake. From adistance, a small island in the lake looks like a pearl floating on the surface of the lake, called Guanghua Island. Taking the island as the boundary northern half of the lake is shaped like a full moon, and the south half lake is shaped like a crescent moon, hence the name.

多千米，有磺溪纵贯其中，沿溪温泉泉眼和地热气喷口密布。温泉区中景观最突出者为北投温瀑和地热

Beitou is the most famous "Hot Springs Village" in Taiwan in the last hundred years, located in the northenmost

谷。北投温瀑位于温泉区北隅，瀑布落差达20余米。瀑布从巨岩直泻而下，飘洒成雾。瀑布颜色微黄，

• 北投温泉区路边水渠内流动的温泉水

（图片提供：FOTOE）

Hot Spring Water Flowing in Ditch by Road Side in Beitou Hot Spring Area

of the city of Taipei, 12 kilometers away from the Taipei downtown area. Hot Springs in Beitou are scattered all over like stars in the sky. The water quality is acidic, containing a large amount of hydrogen sulfide, being sulphur springs, and their temperature is mostly at 40℃ -68℃. Hot spring area is more than 50 kilometers, with sulphur stream running through. Along the stream densely cover hot springs and air vents of geothermal energy. The most prominent landscapes in hot springs zone are Beitou Hot Spring Waterfall and Geothermal Valley. The waterfall is located in the north border of the hot springs area. The fall head of the waterfall is 20 meters. The waterfall makes a sheer drop from a huge rock, swirling into mists. The color of the waterfall is yellowish. Hot-gases are like smoke and steam. The splashed droplets are warm like hot water. Wind around the mountain in the midwood on the side of Beitou Hot Spring Waterfall, until the source, and then get to the Geothermal Valley having won fame both at home and abroad. Looking down at the valley from a high place, you can see a big hole, shaped like a big well, white smoke column of about thirty or forty meters are blown out from the entrance to the

热气若烟若汽，水珠溅起温热若汤，伸手试探，炎热异常。从北投温瀑一侧的密林中盘山而上，直至源头，便到了驰名中外的地热谷。居高俯瞰谷中，可见一个大洞，状若大井，洞口喷出高约三四十米的白烟柱，喷声响若雷霆，声震数里。地热谷水温高达90℃以上，以丝网盛鸡蛋沉于水下，几分钟便可煮熟。因曾有人不慎跌入谷中受烫致死，于是人们“谈谷色变”，给它取名为“地狱谷”。

阳明山温泉与北投温泉并称为“姊妹泉”，在台湾省享有盛誉。阳明山在台北市北郊16千米处，位于大屯山火山群最高峰七星山以南，纱帽山东北，磺溪上游。阳明山原名草山，以多生茅草而得名，后为纪念明代学者王阳明而改名。阳明山温泉位于阳明山风景区内，分前山温泉和后山温泉两部分。泉水终年不歇，水温在70℃以上，水质清澈，呈乳白色，为弱碱性硫化氢泉。温泉周遭尽是醉人的风景，人们在此既可泡温泉，又可欣赏山林美景。

关子岭温泉位于台湾省台南市

cave. The sound is like the thunder, and acoustic shock spreads several *Li*. The water temperature of Geothermal Valley is up to more than 90℃. Put eggs into the water, they are well cooked in a few minutes. There was someone accidentally falling into the valley and being scalded to death, so people turn pale at the mention of the valley, and call it Hell Valley.

Yangming Mountain Hot Spring is known as the Sister Spring with the Beitou Hot Spring, enjoying a high reputation in Taiwan Province. Yangming Mountain is 16 kilometers away from the north suburbs of Taipei City, located in the south of the summit, Qixing (seven stars) Mountain of volcano group in Datun Mountain, and in the northeast of Shamao Mountain and upstream of Huangxi (sulphur creek). Yangming Mountain was originally called Caoshan (grass) Mountain, with the name for its growing many thatches; later the name was changed to commemorate the scholar Wang Yangming in the Ming Dynasty. Yangming Mountain Hot Spring is located in the Yangming Mountain scenic area. There are two parts—front mountain hot spring and back mountain hot spring. Springs do not stop all the year round. The water temperature is above 70℃. The water is clear, assuming ivory-

• **阳明山温泉**（图片提供：曾志/FOTOE）
Yangming Mountain Hot Spring

白河区，四周群山环抱，为台湾南部第一温泉。关子岭还与日本鹿儿岛、意大利西西里岛并列为世界三大泥浆温泉产地。关子岭温泉分为清、浊两穴。浊泉温度约为80℃，色呈浅灰，状似泥汤，为盐类碳

white. It is a weakly alkaline hydrogen sulfide spring. There are intoxicating sceneries all around the hot spring. You can both have a bath in the hot spring and appreciate the beautiful scenery of the mountain forest.

Guanzi Ridge Hot Spring is located

酸泉，有益于神经系统疾病、皮肤病、关节炎等的治疗。清泉温度约为50℃，水质清澈，味甘可饮。

四重溪温泉在台湾省屏东县恒春镇以北约13千米处的莽莽群山之中。这里空气清新宜人，未受污

in the east of Baihe District, Tainan City, Taiwan Province. Surrounded by mountains, it is the first hot spring in southern Taiwan. Guanzi Ridge also stands side by side with Japan's Kagoshima and Sicily in Italy, being the world's three largest places of origin of mud springs. Guanzi Ridge Hot Spring is divided into two caves—clear one and muddy one. The muddy spring temperature is about 80℃; the color is grayish, shaped like hot water with mud, being a salt carbonate spring, and can be used to relieve nervous system diseases, skin disease and arthritis, etc. The clear spring temperature is about 50℃ ; the water is clear and pure, tasting sweet and potable.

Sichong Brook Hot Spring is in vast mountains about 13 kilometers north of Hengchun Town, Pingtung County, Taiwan Province. Here the air is fresh, pleasant and uncontaminated; surroundings are rurality of a piece quiet and beautiful tranquil. Spring water is so clear that people can see the bottom, and it is colorless and tasteless. The water temperature is at 45℃-60℃. This spring can be both drunk and bathed in. In the northeast of the hot spring, there is a famous ancient Shimen battlefield. Two mountains stand facing each other

染，周围是一片清幽恬静的田园风光。泉水清可见底、无色无味，水温在45℃到60℃之间，此泉可饮可浴。温泉的东北方有一处闻名的石门古战场。此地两山夹峙，断崖绝壁，相距仅30余米。一夫据守，万夫莫开，地势险要，故称“石门”。清同治十三年（1874年），日本侵略者在附近登陆进犯，高山族人民曾在此据险抵抗。

here, with broken ridges and steep cliffs, only 30 meters apart. If one man guards the pass, ten thousand are unable to get through. The terrain is strategically situated and difficult of access, so it is called Shimen(a stone-made gate). In the 13th year of the Emperor Tongzhi in the Qing Dynasty (1874), the Japanese aggressors landed and attacked nearby. Gaoshan people formerly resisted the enemy relying on natural barriers.

• **台湾屏东县四重溪温泉区的大众浴池**（图片提供：FOTOE）
Public Bath of Sichong Brook Hot Spring Area in Pingtung County, Taiwan

> 蝴蝶泉

蝴蝶泉坐落在云南省大理市点苍山云弄峰下。这里风光秀丽，泉水清澈，还有天下罕见的奇观——蝴蝶会。蝴蝶泉因此蜚声中外。

蝴蝶泉西靠点苍山，东临洱海，在地下水溶蚀作用下，该地区生成了众多落水洞和溶洞，受大气降水和地表水补给，形成了丰富的岩溶含水层。该含水层中的地下水，沿溶蚀管道流动，溢出地表后形成蝴蝶泉。蝴蝶泉水量稳定，涌水量在18.77升/秒左右。水质优良，矿化度小于0.5克/升，属重碳酸钙镁型水，无色无味。泉池四周用大理石砌成护栏。泉水清澈见底，一串串银白色水泡自沙石中徐徐涌出，汩汩冒出水面，泛起片片水花。

每年农历四月十五前后，云弄

> Butterfly Spring

Butterfly Spring is located at the foot of Yunnong Peak of Diancang Mountain in Dali City, Yunnan Province. There is beautiful scenery with clear spring water, and still the wonders rare in the world—Butterfly Gathering. Consequently, Butterfly Spring becomes famous in China and foreign countries.

Butterfly Spring is near to Diancang Mountain on the west and is close to Erhai Lake on the east. On the dissolution of groundwater, it generats numerous sinkholes and caverns. And because of atmospheric precipitation and surface water recharge, there is a karst aquifer. The groundwater in this aquifer flows along corrosion pipeline, and later overflows to the surface, forming the Butterfly Spring. The seepage water volume is stable, about 18.77 liters per second of high water quality. The

• **蝴蝶泉牌坊**（图片提供：全景正片）

从下关沿滇藏公路北行30余千米，便可以看见一座古色古香的石牌坊。牌坊上的“蝴蝶泉”三个大字，是著名文学家郭沫若（1892—1978）游大理时留下的。

Memorial Archway of Butterfly Spring

Go to north 30 kilometers along the Yunnan-Tibet road from Xiaguan, you can see a memorial archway having an antique flavor. Three characters *Hu Die Quan* (Butterfly Spring) are written on it, which is famous writer Guo Moruo's writing (1892-1978) when he visited Dali and left it.

峰上各种奇花竞相开放，泉边的合欢树散发出一种淡雅的清香，诱使成千上万的蝴蝶前来聚会。这些蝴蝶大的如掌，小的如蜂，或翩舞于花草间，或嬉戏于空中。更有数不清的彩蝶，从合欢树上一只只倒挂下来，结成长串，一直垂到水面，阳光之下，五彩焕然。附近的白族居民都会前来观赏彩蝶，举行聚

mineralization is less than 0.5g/L, belonging to heavy calcium carbonate and magnesium water type, colorless and tasteless. Guard rail is built with the marble around the spring pool. The spring water is so clear that people can see the bottom; strings of silver bubbles slowly gush out from the grit with a gurgle, rippling slices of splashes.

Every year around April 15th of

银苍玉洱

银苍玉洱是指由点苍山和洱海组成的美景。点苍山因山色苍翠、山顶积雪而闻名。点苍山顶上的积雪在夏季消融后，成为此处优质的水源。洱海是一个风光明媚的高原淡水湖泊，素有“高原明珠”之称，形如一弯新月。点苍山和洱海不仅构成了一幅美景，也为蝴蝶等昆虫繁殖与生长提供了优越的环境。

• 点苍山
Diancang Mountain

Yincang Yu'er

Yincang Yu'er indicate the beautiful scenery composed of Diancang Mountain and Erhai Lake. Diancang Mountain is famous for its green mountain color and snows on the top. Snows on the top of Diancang Mountain melt in summer seasons, becoming the waterhead here. Erhai Lake is a plateau freshwater lake with a radiant and enchanting scene, known as the Pearl of the Plateau, shaped like a crescent moon. Diancang Mountain and Erhai Lake not only constitute beautiful scenery, but form a superior environment for insects of butterflies, etc. to breed and grow.

• 洱海
Erhai Lake

会，年轻人也会借此机会寻找意中人。如今蝴蝶会已经成为白族的民间风俗。

• **蝴蝶泉前的合欢树**（图片提供：全景正片）

自古以来，有不少文人学士到蝴蝶泉考察游览，并写下了许多重要的诗文。明代地理学家徐霞客曾在《徐霞客游记》中称颂蝴蝶泉："泉上大树，当四月初，即发花如蛱蝶，须翅栩然，与生蝶无异。又有真蝶千万，连须钩足，自树巅倒悬而下，及于泉面，缤纷络绎，五色焕然。游人俱从此月群而观之，过五月乃已。"清代诗人沙琛在《上关蝴蝶泉》中赞道："迷离蝶树千蝴蝶，衔尾如缨拂翠湉。不到蝶泉谁肯信，幢影幡盖蝶庄严。"

Silk Tree in Front of the Butterfly Spring

Since ancient times, many scholars have been to Butterfly Spring for investigation and tour, and wrote many important poetries. The geographer Xu Xiake in the Ming Dynasty praised Butterfly Spring in his *Xu Xiake's Travel Notes*, "Big trees above the spring bloom like butterflies at the beginning of April. Beards and wings are the same with real butterflies. There are still ten thousand of real butterflies, linking beards and hooking feet, hanging down from the top of the tree to the surface of the spring, vast and various, continuous and bright colorful. Visitors are all delighted at this and watch it in group, which ends after May." The poet Sha Chen in the Qing Dynasty praised in *Shangguan Butterfly Spring*,"Blurred butterfly tree has thousand of butterflies, holding tails in the mouth like tassels to stroke calm green water surface. Who believes if not arriving at Butterfly Spring, butterflies seem solemn with shadow of stone pillars and streamer canopies."

Chinese lunar calendar, all kinds of exotic flowers bloom on Yunnong Peak; silk trees by the spring side exude a kind of elegantly simple delicate fragrance, luring tens of thousands of butterflies come to the party. Among these butterflies, big ones are like the palm and small ones like the bee, either dancing in the flowers and plants or playing in the air. Further, countless butterflies hung upside down from silk trees, forming a long string and hanging down to the surface of the water. Under sunlight, they are bright colorful, spectacular and beautiful. The Bai ethnic group residents nearby will all come to watch butterflies and hold a party. Young people would like to take this opportunity to find lovers, and now the butterfly party has become folk customs of the Bai ethnic group.

大理蝴蝶泉（图片提供：全景正片）

Butterfly Spring in Dali

白族

白族是中国少数民族之一，主要分布在云南、贵州、四川等省。白族使用白语（属汉藏语系），许多白族人也通晓汉语。白族历史悠久，早在公元1世纪前就在以点苍山、洱海和滇池为中心的地区生活。白族文化艺术丰富多彩，张胜温创作的《大理国梵像卷》，被称为“南天瑰宝”。这幅画描绘了774个不一样的人物。笔法精致娴熟、工巧细腻，是中国古代艺术的珍品。白族服饰特点鲜明，以白色为高贵色。白族喜欢烤茶，常用传统的“三道茶”招待贵宾。白族盛大的节日是“三月街”，至今已有上千年历史，每年农历三月十五至三月二十在点苍山下举行。另一个盛大节日是火把节，于农历六月二十四举行。

• 云南大理白族儿童

Children of the Bai Nationality in Dali, Yunnan Province

Bai Ethnic groups

Bai Ethnic groups is one of the Chinese ethnic groups, distributed mainly in provinces of Yunnan, Guizhou and Sichuan. They use Bai Language (belonging to Sino-Tibetan languages; many of them also understand Chinese well. The Bai nationality has a long history. As early as the first century ago, they lived in the region taking Diancang Mountain, Erhai Lake and Dianchi Lake as the center. The culture and art of the Bai ethnic group are rich and colorful. The *Picture Scroll of Figures of the Buddha in Dali* created by Zhang Shengwen is known as south heavenly treasures. The painting depicts 774 different portraits. His calligraphy or drawing is delicate and skilled, exquisite and fine and smooth, which is the ancient Chinese art treasure. Bai's dress characteristic is distinct, taking white as noble. They like to bake tea, and often use traditional *Sandao* Tea (a Bai ethnic tea tradition) to entertain guests. Their grand festival is Sanyue Street (Market Day in March), so far, it has been a history of a thousand years, held at the foot of Diancang Mountain, on every March 15th-20th of the lunar calendar; the other grand festival is the Torch Festival, held on June 24th of the lunar calendar.

> 腾冲泉群

腾冲位于云南省保山市西南部，与缅甸毗邻。这里有中国保存最完好、最壮观的新生代死火山群，有火山70余座，温泉群和温泉点80余处，平均每70平方千米便有一个泉群点，是一座名副其实的地热自然博物馆。

明代地理学家徐霞客于明崇祯十一年至十三年（1638—1640）考察了云南腾冲的众多温泉，在他的《滇游日记》中着墨描写的是硫黄塘（又称“热海大滚锅”）。此泉在县城西南16千米的一个山坳平台的中央，泉池为一个直径3米多、深约1.5米的盆形小池。池底到处喷水冒气，水温达96.6℃，高于当地的沸点95℃。整个水池白浪翻滚、热气腾腾、响声震天，状如沸腾的滚

> Tengchong Spring Groups

Tengchong is located in the southwest of the city of Baoshan, Yunnan Province, adjacent to Burma. Here is China's best preserved and the most spectacular cenozoic extinct volcano group. There are more than 70 volcanos and more than 80 hot spring groups and hot spring points. On an average of every 70 square kilometers, there is a spring group point. So the city which is worthy of the geothermal natural history museum.

The geographer Xu Xiake, in the 11th-13th years of Chongzhen period in the Ming Dynasty (1638-1640), inspected numerous hot springs in the city. What he emphasized to descript in his *Tour Diary in Yunnan* is a large churning cauldron bubble spring of Sulphur Pond (also known as "large hot lake churning cauldron"). This spring is in the center of col platform, 16 kilometers southwest

锅。泉水中含有大量硫黄，空气中有强烈的硫黄味。《徐霞客游记》中有极其生动的描述："遥望其峡中，蒸腾之气，东西数处，郁然勃发，如浓烟卷雾，东濒大溪，西贯山峡……环崖之下，平沙一围，中有孔数百，沸水丛跃，亦如数十人鼓煽于下者……四旁之沙亦热，久立不能停足也。"

硫黄塘西南两千米处，有一个南北走向的小山沟。沟底有一条小溪，小溪两侧是陡峻的崖壁，这里便是黄瓜箐热气沟。热水汽穿沙破

• 腾冲热海
Tengchong Hot Lake

of the county town. The spring pool is a basin shaped small pool, with a diameter of 3 meters and a depth of about 1.5 meters. Water spews and water vapour gives off everywhere in the bottom of the pool. The water temperature is 96.6℃, above the local boiling point 95℃. Whitecaps of the entire pool tumble. Hot-gas is steaming, and sound is earsplitting, shaped like boiling churning cauldron. Spring water contains large amounts of sulfur, with a strong smell of sulphur in the air. Xu Xiake gave a very vivid description, "Overlooking the gorge, one can see several places in east and west suffused with heavy gases that seem as mists Gases approaches the river to the east and run through the gorge to the west···Below the surrounding cliffs, there is a sanaly land with hundreds of pits. The water in the pits is boiling, as if dozens of people are fanning the flames below. The sand around is also hot and people can't stand for a long time. There is a small gully driented south and north which is southwest two kilometers to Sulphur Pond. At the bottom of the gully, there is a small stream; on both sides are steep cliff walls; here is the hot-gas ditch in Cucumber Qing (mountain valley with clumps of trees and bamboos). Hot water gases pass through sands and broken

• 热海大滚锅
Large Hot Lake Churning Cauldron

石，喷涌不息，热气四溢，温度高达95℃。水汽中含有氡等十几种化学元素，当地人往往通过熏蒸的方式，即在泉眼上铺以卵石、沙子，再覆以松针、草席或蓑衣，然后躺在上面，很快就会被热气笼罩，达到身心舒缓的目的。

蛤蟆嘴喷泉距离黄瓜箐热气沟约数百米。它是悬崖上的一个岩峰，外形似蛤蟆嘴，每隔几秒钟就会喷出两股五尺多高的水柱，水温达95℃。

腾冲的泉群种类复杂，除了沸泉、地热蒸气泉外，还有喷泉、巨泉，以及令人闻风丧胆的毒气泉、硫酸泉等。喷泉里的高温、高压水

stones, spewing off without break, hot gas overflowing; the temperature is up to 95℃. The water gas contains more than ten kinds of chemical elements, such as radon, etc. Local people often use fumigation manner, i.e. laying gravel and sand, then covered with pine needles, grassmat or straw rain cape; after that people lay down on it, and will be soon enveloped by hot-gases for relaxation.

Toad Mouth Geyser is about hundreds of meters apart from the hot-gas ditch in Huangguaqing. It is from a rock peak on the cliff, like a toad mouth. Every few seconds, two waterspouts would spout to a height of more than one meter, with a water temperature of 95℃.

Tengchong spring groups are complex in categories, in addition to boiling springs, geothermal steam springs, and there are still geysers, giant springs, as well as poison gas springs, and sulphuric acid springs making people a tremble with fear on hearing of, etc. High-temperature and high-pressure hydrothermal steam of the geyser in Tengchong jet out from the circular small holes, one meter high off the ground, again sprinkle down one after another, like fireworks spray in all directions. Giant spring is known for its huge amount of gushing water; the water

热蒸气从圆形小孔中喷射而出，能离地一米多高，再纷纷洒落，如礼花四射。巨泉以涌水量巨大而得名，水温一般高出常温2℃—3℃，四季不变，其热流量占整个腾冲地区的三分之一。县城东北曲石附近有一处被人们称为“扯雀塘”的毒气泉，泉内能喷出一氧化碳和硫化氢，其喷气孔附近常见被毒死的老鼠和雀鸟。硫酸泉热气腾腾，到处是嗞嗞的响声，地表砂石裸露、寸草不生，人们不敢涉足，是天然的“禁区”。

temperature is generally 2℃-3℃ higher than normal temperature, and invariant at all seasons; the rate of heat flow takes 1/3 of the entire Tengchong region. There is a spring called Cheque (pull sparrow) Pond in the northwest of County, which is a poison gas spring. It can blow out carbon monoxide and hydrogen sulfide; poisoned mice, sparrows and birds are often seen near air injection holes. Sulphuric acid spring has steaming hot-gases; everywhere is hissing sound; uncovered dinas is on the earth's surface; not even a blade of grass grows. People dare not set foot in; it is a a natural "forbidden zone".

• 腾冲荷花乡坝派巨泉（图片提供：FOTOE）
Bapai Giant Spring in Lotus Township, Tengchong

> 华清池

华清池位于陕西省西安市临潼区南骊山西北麓，故也叫“骊山温泉”。千百年来，以其旖旎的风光、众多的古迹和温滑的泉水蜚声中外。

华清池是中国有据可查的最早用于医疗的温泉之一。西周（前1046—前771）时，周幽王曾在这里建过“骊宫”，用以疗养。秦始皇时，又在此建造殿宇，砌石成池，赐名“骊山汤”。唐贞观十八年（644年），此地建起“汤泉宫”，天宝六年（747年），再次扩建。骊山上亭台楼阁错落，曲道回廊相连。泉池置于豪华的宫殿楼阁之内，宫殿改称“华清宫”。因宫殿建在泉池之上，故泉池称“华清池”。唐玄宗和杨贵妃每于冬季居此。

> Huaqing Hot Spring

Huaqing Hot Spring is located at the northwest foot of Lishan Mountain in the south of Lintong District, Xi'an City, Shaanxi Province, so it is also called Lishan Hot Spring. For centuries, it has become famous in China and foreign countries for its beautiful scenery, numerous historic sites and warm slippery spring water.

Huaqing Hot Spring is one of the hot springs used in the earliest medical treatment, which was recorded in ancient China. During the Western Zhou Dynasty (1046 B.C.-771 B.C.), King You of Zhou formerly built Ligong Palace here, used for health care. During the reign of the First Emperor of the Qin Dynasty, palaces were built here; a poll was built by laying stones, and the name was granted Lishan Hot Spring. In the 18th year of Zhenguan period in the Tang

• **西安华清池**
Huaqing Hot Spring, Xi'an

华清宫因唐玄宗和杨贵妃而负盛名。华清池向西，有被称为“九龙汤”的浴池，是当年唐玄宗入浴的御汤。浴池中立有一双用白玉雕成的莲花，从莲花中喷出清澈的泉水，似碎琼乱玉。九龙汤以西是杨

Dynasty (644), "Hot Spring Palace" was built here, and in the 6th year of Tianbao period (747), it was expanded again, hence pavilions, terraces, and towers are scattered randomly on Lishan Mountain, and connected with crooked paths and winding corridors, and the spring was placed in the grand palaces and towers, renamed Huaqing Palace. Because the palace is built on the spring pond, it is called Huaqing Hot Spring. At that time, every winter, Emperor Xuanzong of the Tang Dynasty and Yang Guifei (highest-ranking imperial concubine) would take up residence here.

Huaqing Palace has long enjoyed a good reputation because of Emperor Xuanzong of the Tang Dynasty and Yang Guifei. On the west of the Huaqing Hot Spring is a bathing pool called Nine-dragon Hot Spring, which is a royal hot spring for Emperor Xuanzong of the Tang Dynasty to have a bath in those days. In the bathing pool, there stands a pair of lotuses carved with white jade; clear spring water spout from the lotuses, like white snow. On the west of Nine-dragon Hot Spring is the Royal Pool for Yang Guifei to have a bath, shaped like a flower of crabapple called Haitang (crabapple) Spring. The poet Bai Juyi

• 贵妃池遗址
Royal Pool Site

• 九龙汤遗址
Nine-dragon Hot Spring Site

• **太子汤遗址**

太子汤是专供太子沐浴的汤池。

Site of Crown Prince Hot Spring

The Crown Prince Hot Spring is the hot spring pond for crown prince to have a bath.

贵妃沐浴的贵妃池，因形状似海棠花又称“海棠汤”。唐代诗人白居易在《长恨歌》里描写的“春寒赐浴华清池，温泉水滑洗凝脂。侍儿扶起娇无力，始是新承恩泽时”便是杨贵妃沐浴后的娇态。

in the Tang Dynasty described, in his *Song of Eternal Sorrow*, the coquettish behavior after Yang Guifei having a bath, "One cold spring day, she was ordered to bathe in the Huaqing Hot Spring. The warm water slipped down her glistening jade-like body. When her maids helped her rise, she looked so frail and lovely. At once, she won the emperor's flavor."

唐玄宗与杨贵妃

唐玄宗，又称“唐明皇”，是中国历史上著名的皇帝之一。他在位期间开创了唐朝最为鼎盛的时期，史称“开元盛世”。他与杨贵妃的爱情故事通过白居易的《长恨歌》而千古传诵。

杨贵妃是中国古代四大美女之一，因才貌双全，受到唐玄宗的百般宠爱，她的家族也因而得到唐玄宗的厚待。为了讨杨贵妃的欢心，唐玄宗费尽心机。杨贵妃爱吃南方产的新鲜荔枝，唐玄宗就命人快马加鞭从南方运到华清宫，以此博红颜一笑。唐玄宗晚年不理朝政，只顾与杨贵妃游乐，朝政每况愈下。加上杨贵妃的堂兄杨国忠操纵朝政，败坏政事。后范阳节度使安禄山以诛杨国忠为名，发动叛乱，史

• 西安华清池中的杨贵妃雕像
Statue of Yang Guifei in Huaqing Hot Spring in Xi'an

称“安史之乱”。唐玄宗带着杨贵妃逃出皇宫。至马嵬驿，士兵哗变，杀掉杨国忠，并逼唐玄宗赐死杨贵妃。唐玄宗无奈，只得缢死杨贵妃。

• 《华清出浴图》康涛（清）

Picture of Huaqing Bathing, by Kang Tao (Qing Dynasty, 1616-1911)

Emperor Xuanzong of the Tang Dynasty and Yang Guifei

Emperor Xuanzong of the Tang Dynasty, also known as Tang Minghuang, who is one of the famous emperors in the Chinese history. During his reign, he initiated the most prosperous period in the Tang Dynasty, known as the Kaiyuan Heyday Period. The love story of him and Yang Guifei passed down through the ages by Bai Juyi's *Song of Eternal Sorrow*.

Yang Guifei is one of the Top Four Beauties in Ancient China. Both beautiful and highly gifted, she received the love of Emperor Xuanzong in every possible way, and her family was treated kindly and generously by Emperor Xuanzong. In order to ask for the favor of Yang Guifei, Emperor Xuanzong taxed his ingenuity. Yang liked southern fresh leechee, so Emperor Xuanzong ordered people to transport them from the south to Huaqing Palace at the fastest speed, and tried to win a smile from her. Emperor Xuanzong ignored affairs of state in his old age, and was absorbed in playing with Yang Guifei; affairs of state went from bad to worse. And Yang Guifei's cousin, Yang Guozhong's embezzlement and corruption led to the situation getting out of hand. The Fanyang *Jiedushi* (governor of one or more provinces in charge of both civil and military affairs during the Tang Dynasty) An Lushan led a military mutiny on the pretext of killing Yang Guozhong, historyically known as An Shi Rebellion. Emperor Xuanzong took Yang Guifei to escape from the palace. At Mawei Post, soldiers mutinied, killed Yang Guozhong, and forced Emperor Xuanzong to grant suicide to Yang Guifei. Emperor Xuanzong had to hang Yang Guifei in the end.

华清池的热量主要源于地球内部已经冷凝或者正在冷凝的岩浆所散发的热量。附近岩层的部分矿物成分在地下热水的活动过程中受到溶解，形成矿泉，在断裂带处出露地表。华清池的温泉共有四处泉眼，水温43℃，总流量约为110吨/时，矿化度低，富含氡、硅、氟、铁、锂、锶、钡、钾、钠、钙、碘、溴、硼等微量元素，具有消肿去毒、润肤去疾的功能。

The geothermal energies of Huaqing Hot Spring mainly originate from the waste heat sent out by magma which under the deep underground, has already condensed or is condensing. Part of the mineral compositions of nearby stratum dissolves in the process of underground hot-water activities, forming mineral springs, which are exposed to earth's surface from the fracture zone. Huaqing Hot Spring has four mouths in all; the water temperature is 43℃; the total flow is about 110 tons/ hour, with a low degree of mineralization, containing rich trace elements, e.g. radon, silicon, fluorine, iron, lithium, strontium, barium, potassium, sodium, calcium, iodine, bromine, boron, etc., having the function of detumescence, detoxification, moisturizing and abolishing diseases.

> 月牙泉

月牙泉位于甘肃省敦煌市区南7千米鸣沙山北麓。月牙泉古称“沙井”，俗名“药泉”，其轮廓形似一弯新月，因而得名，有“沙漠第一泉”之称。月牙泉澄澈如镜，泉水清冽甘美，池旁水草丛生，芦苇摇曳，蓝天黄沙，碧水绿树，清幽雅致。

据文献记载，月牙泉在汉代时便已闻名。千百年来流沙堆积，泉水却从未干涸，实为自然界的奇观。相传泉中生长有铁背鱼和七星草，人吃后可以消灾祛病、延年益寿，因而民间又称其为“药泉”。历史上泉旁曾建有药王庙，自汉代起，每年端午节，人们纷至沓来，登沙山，观泉景，饮浴泉水，相沿成习。

> Crescent Spring

Crescent Spring is located in the north foot of Mingsha Mountain, 7 kilometers to the south of Dunhuang City, Gansu Province. In ancient times, the Crescent Spring is called "Sand Well", with a trivial name "Medicinal Spring". Its outline resembles a crescent moon, hence the name, and it is called The No.1 Spring in Desert. It is as clear as a mirror; the spring water is clear, pleasant and tasty. Nearby the pond, sweeds grow thickly, bulrushes sway, with blue sky and yellow sand, blue water and green plants, being quiet and beautiful refined.

According to literature, Crescent Spring was famous in the Han Dynasty. For thousands of years, drift sands have accumulated, but the spring water have never dried up, really the wonder of nature. According to legend, Tiebei (iron back) fishes and Qixing (seven stars)

敦煌莫高窟

莫高窟位于甘肃省敦煌市城区东南25千米处的鸣沙山东麓，开凿于公元5世纪至14世纪之间，至今仍完好地保存着从北魏到元代的洞窟492个，壁画4.5万多平方米，彩塑3000余尊，唐宋木构窟檐5座。1900年在莫高窟偶然发现的藏经洞中藏有从公元4世纪至14世纪的历代文物五六万件，这是20世纪初中国考古历史上的一次重大发现，震惊了世界。

• 敦煌莫高窟（图片提供：全景正片）
Dunhuang Mogao Grottoes

莫高窟集多彩的建筑、石刻、壁画、彩塑艺术于一体，是世界上规模最庞大、内容最丰富、历史最悠久的佛教艺术宝库，1987年被列入《世界遗产名录》。世界遗产委员会评价其“不仅是东西方贸易的中转站，同时也是宗教、文化和知识的交汇处……以其雕像和壁画闻名于世，展示了延续千年的佛教艺术”。

Mogao Grottoes of Dunhuang

Mogao Grottoes is located at the eastern foot of Mingsha Mountain, which is 25 km southeast of the urban area of Dunhuang City, Gansu Province. It was dug between the fifth century and fourteenth century. So far, 492 Grottoes from the Northern Wei Dynasty to the Yuan Dynasty have been still preserved in good order; there are frescos of more than 45 thousand square meters, more than 3000 colored sculptures and 5 wooden canopy structure caves. In 1900, a cave for preserving Buddhist sutra was incidentally found at Mogao Grottoes, in possession of fifty thousand or sixty thousand cultural relics of successive dynasties from fourth century to fourteenth century. It is a great discovery in Chinese archaeology history at the beginning of twentieth century, which shocked the world.

The Mogao Grottoes collect colorful buildings, stone carvings, frescos and painted sculpture art all in one. It is the world's Buddhist art treasury with hugest scale, most abundant content and age-old history. In 1987, it was taken into the World Heritage List. The World Heritage Committee appraised it is "not only the East-West trade freight transfer station, but also the intersection of religion, cultural and intellectual···It is world-famous with its statues and frescos, showing the Buddhist art lasted for thousand years".

月牙泉处于鸣沙山流沙的怀抱中，这种沙山与泉水共生的现象在自然界并不多见，但是二者却和谐地结合在一起，构成了奇特的景观。这是因为月牙泉附近的疏勒河的河水从地下渗流到此地，在良好的隔水层上形成了丰富的含水层。含水层一旦出现裂隙，水就会由于压力的作用上涌，形成裂隙泉。而月牙泉也正是因为鸣沙山脚下的一道裂隙而形成。月牙泉的北、西、南三面环山，仅有东面是风口。当

grasses grew in the spring. When eating them, people can eliminate misfortunes and diseases and prolong life, thus it is also known as "Medicinal Spring" among the people. In history Yaowang (King of Medicine) Temple was formerly built beside the spring. Since the Han Dynasty, every May on the Dragon Boat Festival, people have come in a throng, ascending dune, visiting spring view and drinking and bathing water, which become a custom through long time usage.

Crescent Spring is embraced by

• **敦煌月牙泉**（图片提供：全景正片）
Crescent Spring of Dunhuang

• 月牙泉旁的月牙阁（图片提供：全景正片）
Crescent Tower Next to the Crescent Spring

风从东面吹来时，气流受到沙山阻挡只能在山中旋转上升，把山下的细沙带到了山顶，失去了形成流沙的条件。所以，月牙泉历经几千年却未被流沙埋没，形成了沙泉共存的奇特美景。

shifting sands of Mingsha Mountain. The symbiotic phenomenon of sand hills and springs is few and far between in nature, but the two are a harmonious combination, forming a unique landscape. This is because Shule river water near the Crescent Spring is seepage from the underground to here, forming abundant aquifers on satisfactory water-resisting layer. Once aquifer appears cracks, water will upwell owing to the pressure function, forming fissure springs. Crescent Spring is also formed precisely because of a crack at the foot of Mingsha Mountain. Crescent Spring is ringed on three sides, north, west and south by mountains; only on east side is the wind gap. When the wind blows from the east, the air flow is obstructed by the dune only to revolve and rise in mountains, taking silver sands below mountains to mountaintops, and losing the condition to form drift sands. So, Crescent Spring has not been buried by drift sands through thousands of years, forming peculiar beautiful scenery of coexistence of sands and springs.

> 酒泉

酒泉在甘肃省酒泉市东关区。酒泉市因酒泉而得名，其位于祁连山主峰之下，河西走廊西部，南望祁连山，北通沙漠，东迎华岳，西达伊吾，为历代的边防重镇，兵家必争之地。酒泉古城已有1600多年的历史，自古以产玉杯而负盛名。唐代诗人王翰的诗作《凉州词》传唱古今："葡萄美酒夜光杯，欲饮琵琶马上催。醉卧沙场君莫笑，古来征战几人回？"

尽管河西走廊干旱少雨，但祁连山区却有较丰富的降水。四周高山上的积雪在夏季也会消融。在酒泉地区，冰雪融水同祁连山的大气降水汇成北大河、洪水河等内陆河流，下注河西走廊，许多泉眼出露在河流冲（洪）积扇的边缘。酒泉

> Jiuquan Spring

Jiuquan Spring is in the east pass of Jiuquan City, Gansu Province. Jiuquan City gets its name for the Jiuquan Spring, located below the highest peak of Qilian Mountains, in the westward of Hexi Corridor. On the south is Qilian Mountains, on the north is a desert, on the west are Huashan Mountain and Yueshan Mountain, and on the west is Yiwu County. It is a border defense strategic town and a military hotly contested spot of past dynasties. The ancient city of Jiuquan has a history of over 1600 years, and it has been known for exquisite jade cups since ancient times. The poet Wang Han's poem *Liangzhou Tune* in the Tang Dynasty has been popular until now, "Good grape wine in the noctilucent winecup, wishing to drink but pipa being immediately remindered. Don't sneer if the warriors drunk lying on the battlefield.

甘肃祁连山下
At the Foot of Qilian Mountains, Gansu Province

便位于祁连山冲（洪）积扇前部，恰居地下水的溢出带。

酒泉古称“金泉”，相传古代有人在泉边饮水时，发现水中有金光，循着金光找到了金子，故名“金泉”。史籍中载：“城下有金泉，其味如酒。”汉武帝元狩二年（前121年），为打通与西域间的交通，派遣骠骑将军霍去病远征河西，大破匈奴，同年置酒泉郡。传

• **霍去病雕像**

霍去病（前140—前117），中国西汉杰出的军事家。

Statue of Huo Qubing

Huo Qubing (140 B.C.-117 B.C.), an excellent strategist of the Western Han Dynasty, China.

How many soldiers have ever come back from the battlefield since ancient times?"

Although there is little rain in the Hexi Corridor, Qilian Mountains has abundant precipitation. All around the mountains are covered with snow, melting in the summer. In the Jiuquan area, meltwater and Qilian Mountains' atmospheric precipitation merge into inland rivers, e.g. the North Great River and Flood River. Downward flow in the Hexi Corridor, many springs exposed at the edge of river alluvial fans and proluvial fans. Jiuquan Spring is located in the leading edge of river alluvial fans and proluvial fans of Qilian Mountains; exactly sits on the overflow zone of underground water.

Jiuquan Spring was called Golden Spring in ancient times. According to legend, people in ancient times drank water by the spring and saw golden light in the water.Following the golden light he found gold, so named Golden Spring. According to historical records, "Downward the city, there is a golden spring; its taste is like wine." In the second year of the Yuanshou period (121 B.C.) of the Emperor Wu of the Han Dynasty, in order to get through the traffic with the Western Regions, he dispatched General Huo Qubing for Hexi expedition,

酒泉玉

酒泉玉产于酒泉附近的祁连山中，故又名“祁连玉”。其开采历史可上溯至新石器时代。齐家文化时期（约公元前2000年）的甘肃武威皇娘娘台遗址，曾出土过以酒泉玉制成的精美玉璧。

按产地分，酒泉玉有乐都的中坝玉、湟中的丹麻玉、海西的柴达木玉等。按矿物成分的不同，酒泉玉分为以蛇纹石为主的蛇纹玉，以透闪石、淡斜绿泥石为主的酒泉软玉，以钙铝榴石、透辉石、斜长石等为主的翠玉、白玉等。

酒泉玉的外观多呈浅绿、翠绿、墨绿、白等颜色，结构致密，半透明，硬度为摩氏4—7。

• 酒泉玉制成的夜光杯（图片提供：FOTOE）
Noctilucent Winecup Made of Jiuquan Jade

Jiuquan Jade

Jiuquan jade is produced in Qilian Mountains near Jiuquan, so it is also known as Qilian jade. The mining history can be traced back to the Neolithic Age. During the Qijia Culture period (about 2000 B.C.), in imperial Niangniang stage site in Wuwei, Gansu Province, exquisite jade *Bi* (a round flat piece of jade with a hole in its centre, used for ceremonial purposes in ancient China) made of Jiuquan jade have been excavated.

According to the place of origin, Jiuquan jade is divided into Zhongba jade of Ledu, Danma jade of Huangzhong and Chaidamu jade of Haixi, etc. According to mineral ingredients, it is divided into serpentine-jade giving priority to serpentine, Jiuquan Jade nephrite giving priority to grammatite and leuchtenbergite, blue jade and white jade giving priority to grossular, diopside and plagioclase, etc.

The appearances of Jiuquan jade are mostly in light green, jade green, blackish green and white, etc., with compact structure, translucent texture. The hardness is 4-7 on Mohs scale.

说霍去病率兵打败匈奴后，汉武帝为表彰他的战功，派使者从长安运来御酒10瓶，犒赏将士。当时将士

shattering the Huns. In the same year, Jiuquan Prefecture was set up. It was said that after Huo Qubing leading the army

有20万，但御酒仅有10瓶。霍去病想出了一个妙法，将10瓶御酒倒进金泉中，当即泉水化为美酒，饮之不竭。与将士们开怀共饮，从此“酒泉”之名盛传开来。

酒泉原有泉眼三处，其中两个早已干涸，现仅存一眼。如今泉边砌起了水磨石的圆形围栏，汩汩的泉水汇成一米多深的澄碧清亮的水潭。泉眼里咕嘟咕嘟冒出的大水泡，如同串串珍珠。酒泉每昼夜涌水量约500立方米。泉水矿化度低，水温在10℃—30℃，冬季不寒，夏季清凉，宜饮用，是干旱地区难得的生活、生产用水。

• 酒泉公园内的碑亭（图片提供：FOTOE）
Stela Pavilion in Jiuquan Park

and defeating the Huns, Emperor Wu of the Han Dynasty sent messengers to transport 10 bottles of royal wine from Chang'an to reward soldiers. There were 200,000 soldiers, but only 10 bottles of the royal wine. Huo Qubing thought of a dodge, poured 10 bottles of the royal wine into the Golden Spring; immediately spring turned into good wine. It was inexhaustible to drink. Huo and the soldiers drank to their content. From then on, the name of Jiuquan Spring was widely known.

The original Jiuquan Spring had three mouths two of which dried up long ago. Now there is only one remained. Now, terrazzo circular enclosures have been built by the spring side; gurgling spring water gathers together into an azure clear swag of 1.5-1.6 meters deep. Big water vacuoles keep bubbling up from the mouth of the spring, like strings of pearls. The gushing water yield of Jiuquan Spring is about 500 cubic meters every day and night. Mineralization degree of the spring water is low. The water temperature is at 10℃-30℃; it is not cold in winter, and is cool and refreshing in summer, and suitable for drinking. It is precious for domestic water and production water supply in an arid region.

> 羊八井地热田

羊八井地热田位于西藏自治区拉萨市西北约90千米当雄县境羊八井区西侧。西藏的地热资源丰富，地热活动强烈，中国其他省区难以与其相比。其地热类型有20多种，有温泉、热泉、沸泉、热水塘、沸泥塘，还有奇特罕见的间歇泉、爆炸泉及热水河。其中最著名的为羊八井，此处有沸泉、喷气孔和冒气的地面。

西藏有地热由来已久，较早的文献记载有唐代的《法苑珠林》，其中《王玄策行传》云："吐蕃国西南有一涌泉，平地涌出，激水高五六尺，甚热，煮肉即熟，气上冲天，像似气雾。"王玄策为唐太宗时期的右卫率府长史，三次出使印度，这段历史记载便是他途经吐蕃

> Yangbajing Geothermal Field

Yangbajing Geothermal Field is located in the west side of Yangbajain area in Dangxiong County, which is 90 km northwest of Lhasa City, Xizang Autonomous Region. Tibet is rich in geothermal resources, and the geothermal activity is intense. Other Chinese provinces and regions are unable to compare with it. There are more than 20 geothermal types, e.g. warm springs, hot springs, boiling springs, hot water ponds, bubbling mud ponds, the unique rare geyser, explosion springs and hot river. Yangbajing Geothermal Field is the most famous among them, with boiling springs, fumaroles and steaming ground.

Geothermal energy in Xizang has a long histy. *Collection of Gems of Buddhist Literature Center* of the Tang Dynasty

（今西藏）时所见的地热景象。

羊八井处于山谷盆地内，两侧为海拔五六千米的高山，山顶终年积雪。羊八井地区分布着数十处高热间歇性喷泉，最高水温达92℃，远高于当地沸点86℃。高温间歇性喷泉是在特定条件下，地下高温热水周期性地水汽转化，在泉口间断地喷出大量水汽混合物而形成的。羊八井地热田东北有一个面积约7350平方米、深达16米的热水湖。湖水清澈湛蓝，热水喷涌，温度常年保持在50℃左右。

• 西藏羊八井（图片提供：全景正片）
Tibet Yangbajing

is the earlier document records, among which *Wang Xuance Journey Biography* says, "There is a gushing spring in the southwest of Tubo. It pours out from flat ground; splashed water is around 2 meters high. The water is so hot that can soonly cook meat. Gases soar to the heaven, like aerial fog." Wang Xuance was Zhangshi (an official in charge of historical record in the ancient times) of *Right Chief Military Commissions* during the reign of Emperor Taizong of the Tang Dynasty, being sent on a diplomatic mission to India three times. The words described the geothermal scene that he saw passing through Tubo.

Yangbajing Geothermal field is in a valley basin, on both sides are high mountains of five or six kilometers above sea level.Yangbajing area is dotted with dozens of high temperature geysers. The maximum temperature is up to 92℃, far above the local boiling point of 86. High temperature geyser is formed under specific conditions. Underground hot water seasonally converts between water and vapour, so the mouth of spring can spew a large number of intermittence steam and water mixture. In the northeast of Yangbajing Geothermal Field, there is a hot-water lake of an area of 7350

• 羊八井地热发电站（图片提供：全景正片）
Yangbajing Geothermal Power Station

羊八井盆地下面埋藏着温度高、厚度大的地热储层，最高温度达172℃。据估计，仅羊八井地热浅层的热能，至少可发电15万千瓦时。目前，羊八井地热田已经建成了30多口蒸气喷井，安装了发电机组，在拉萨市的电网中发挥了重要作用。

square meters, and 16 meters deep. The lake water is clear and azure blue; hot water is spurting out. The temperature all the year round maintains at about 50℃.

Under the Yangbajing Basin are buried underground heat reservoir strata with high temperature and thickness; the maximum temperature is up to 172℃. According to estimates, the Yangbajing geothermal shallow heat storage resources can at least generate electricity of 150 thousand kilowatts. At present, in the Yangbajing Geothermal Field, people have built more than 30 steam injection wells, and installed generating sets, which plays an important role in Lhasa power grid.